Presents

ACOUSTIC GUITAR COURSE BOOK
EXPANDED EDITION

Written & Method By:
John McCarthy

Adapted By: Jimmy Rutkowski
Supervising Editor: Joe Palombo
Music Transcribing & Engraving: Jimmy Rutkowski
Production Manager: Joe Palombo
Layout, Graphics & Design: Jimmy Rutkowski
Photography: Jimmy Rutkowski, Rodney Dabney
Copy Editors: Cathy McCarthy, Alex Palombo

Cover Art Direction & Design:
Jimmy Rutkowski

HL14041785
ISBN: 978-1-4584-5969-5
Produced by The Rock House Method®

Table of Contents

About the Author

John McCarthy
Creator of
the Rock House Method

John is the creator of **The Rock House Method**®, the world's leading musical instruction system. Over his 20 year career, he has produced and/or appeared in more than 100 instructional products. Millions of people around the world have learned to play music using John's easy to follow, accelerated program.

John is a virtuoso guitarist who has worked with some of the industry's most legendary musicians. He has the ability to break down, teach and communicate music in a manner that motivates and inspires others to achieve their dreams of playing an instrument.

As a guitarist and songwriter, John blends together a unique style of Rock, Metal, Funk and Blues in a collage of melodic compositions, jam-packed with masterful guitar techniques. His sound has been described as a combination of vintage guitar rock with a progressive, gritty edge that is perfectly suited for today's audiences.

Throughout his career, John has recorded and performed with renowned musicians like Doug Wimbish (who has worked with Joe Satriani, Living Colour, The Rolling Stones, Madonna, Annie Lennox and many more top flight artists), Grammy winner Leo Nocentelli, Rock & Roll Hall of Fame inductees Bernie Worrell and Jerome "Big Foot" Brailey, Freekbass, Gary Hoey, Bobby Kimball, David Ellefson (founding member of seven time Grammy nominee Megadeth), Will Calhoun (who has worked with B.B. King, Mick Jagger and Paul Simon), Jordan Giangreco from the acclaimed band The Breakfast, and solo artist Alex Bach. John has also shared the stage with Blue Oyster Cult, Randy Bachman, Marc Rizzo, Jerry Donahue, Bernard Fowler, Stevie Salas, Brian Tichy, Kansas, Al Dimeola and Dee Snyder.

For more information on John, his music and his instructional products visit www.rockhousemethod.com.

CREATING MUSICIANS
ONE LESSON AT A TIME

Introduction

Welcome to **The Rock House Method®** system of learning. You are joining millions of aspiring musicians around the world who use our easy-to-understand methods for learning to play music.

Unlike conventional learning programs, The Rock House Method® is a four-part teaching system that employs DVD, backing tracks and 24/7 online lesson support along with this book to give you a variety of sources to assure a complete learning experience. The products can be used individually or together. The DVD's that come with this book match the curriculum exactly, providing you with a live instructor for visual reference. In addition, the DVD's contain some valuable extras like sections on changing your strings, guitar care and an interactive chord library.

How to Use the Lesson Support Site

Every Rock House product offers FREE membership to our interactive *Lesson Support* site. Use the member number included with your book to register at www.rockhousemethod.com. You will find your member number on the sleeve that contains your DVD's. Once registered, you can use this fully interactive site along with your product to enhance your learning experience, expand your knowledge, link with instructors, and connect with a community of people around the world who are learning to play music using The Rock House Method®. There are sections that directly correspond to this product within the Additional Information and Backing Tracks sections. There are also a variety of other tools you can utilize such as Ask The Teacher, Quizzes, Reference Material, Definitions, Forums, Live Chats, Guitar Professor and much more.

Icon Key

Throughout this book, you'll periodically notice the following icons. They indicate when there are additional learning tools available on our support website for the section you're working on. When you see an icon in the book, visit the member section of www.rockhousemethod.com for musical backing tracks, additional information and learning utilities.

Backing Track Number

There are accompanying backing tracks and audio demonstrations available for you to download from the *Lesson Support* site at www.rockhousemethod.com. When you see this backing track icon in the book note the track number that will correspond with the lesson. We have divided the tracks into two audio CD partitions as recommended for burning onto disc.

Additional Information

The question mark icon indicates there is more information for that section available on the website. It can be theory, more playing examples, or tips.

Metronome

Metronome icons are placed next to the examples that we recommend you practice using a metronome. You can download a free, adjustable metronome from our support site.

Tablature

This icon indicates that there is additional guitar tablature available on the website that corresponds to the lesson. There is also an extensive database of music online that is updated regularly.

Tuner

Also found on the website is a free online tuner that you can use to help you tune your instrument.

CHAPTER I
Parts of the Guitar

The guitar is divided into three main sections: the body, the neck and the headstock. The assembly that anchors the strings to the body is called the bridge. The bridge pins are the string pegs that secure the strings to the bridge, and the saddle holds them properly in place. On many guitars, the height of the strings (or *action*) can be adjusted using the saddle. The sound hole on the body projects the sound from the guitar. Some guitars also have a pick guard to protect the wood from getting scratched by the pick. At the end of the body is the strap button where a guitar strap can be attached. The front face of the neck is called the fretboard (or *fingerboard*). The metal bars going across the fretboard are called frets. The dots are position markers (or *fret markers*) for visual reference to help you gauge where you are on the neck while playing. The nut is the string guide that holds the strings in place where the neck meets the headstock. The headstock contains the machine heads (also referred to as *tuners*); the machine heads are used to tune the strings by tightening or loosening them.

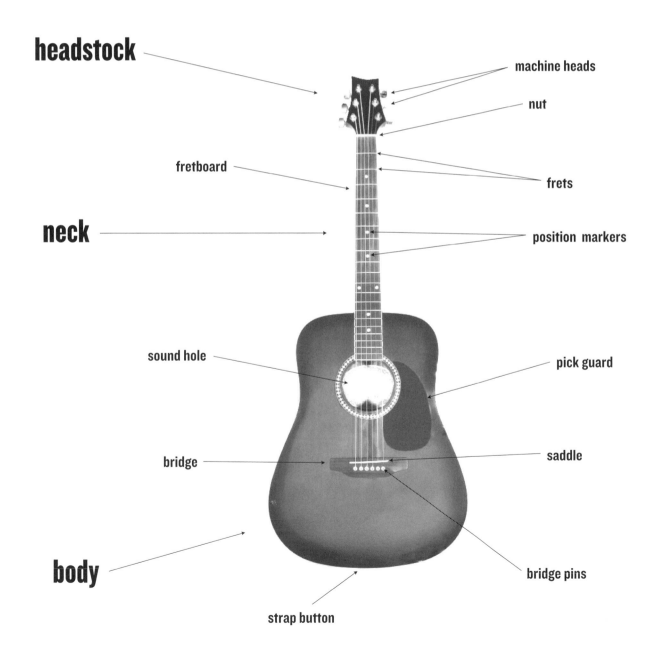

Holding the Guitar

The photos below show the proper way to hold a guitar. You can rest the body of the guitar on your right or left leg - either way is correct. Certain styles of music may be played more comfortably one way or the other. Experiment with it and decide which way feels more natural.

Throughout this book we will refer to the picking hand as your right hand and the hand fretting the notes as your left hand. If you are left handed and playing a left handed guitar, just make the necessary adjustments as you follow along (read "right hand" to mean your left hand and vice versa).

Holding the guitar.

Popular way of holding the acoustic guitar for strumming songs.

For classical style and fingerpicking, you can rest the guitar on your left leg (between your legs) to tilt the neck up and provide added control.

Holding the Pick

Hold the pick between the index finger and thumb of your right hand. Leave just the tip pointing out, perpendicular to your thumb. Your thumb and finger should be placed in the center of the pick, grasping it firmly to give you good control. Leave your hand open (don't make a fist) and let the rest of your fingers hang loosely.

Grasp the pick between your index finger and thumb.

Leave your hand open and your other fingers loose.

To properly position the pick, center the pick on your index finger (Fig. 1) and bring your thumb down on top of it (Fig. 2). Pinch your thumb and finger together and leave just the tip of the pick showing (Fig. 3).

Fig. 1

Fig. 2

Fig. 3

Right Hand Position

Place your right arm on the very top of the guitar and let it drape down almost parallel to the bridge (Fig. 4). Leave part of your hand or fingers touching the guitar's body and keep them anchored to the guitar (Fig. 5). This will help give your picking hand a reference point.

Fig. 4

Fig. 5

Left Hand Position

Hold your left hand out in front of you with your wrist straight (Fig. 6). Curl your fingers in and just naturally bring your hand back to the neck of the guitar (Figs. 7 & 8). Try not to bend or contort your wrist. Your fingers should stay curled inward; most of the time only your fingertips will touch the strings when playing. The first joint of your thumb should be in the middle of the back of the neck (Fig. 9). Try to avoid touching the neck with any other part of your hand. Make sure you have the proper right and left hand positions down so that when we progress you'll have no problems.

Fig. 6

Fig. 7

Fig. 8

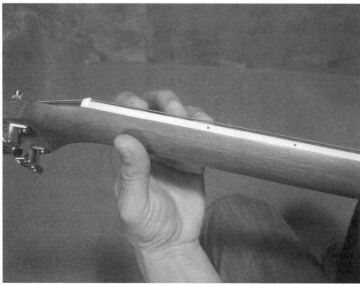

Fig. 9

Tuning

Each of the six strings on a guitar is tuned to and named after a different note (*pitch*). The thinnest or 1st string is referred to as the highest string because it is the *highest sounding* string. The thickest or 6th string is referred to as the lowest string because it is the *lowest sounding* string. Memorize the names of the open strings. These notes form the basis for finding any other notes on the guitar.

Names of the Open Strings

6th string	5th string	4th string	3rd string	2nd string	1st string
E	A	D	G	B	E

6th string (thickest)
lowest sounding string

1st string (thinnest)
highest sounding string

Tune your guitar using the machine heads on the headstock. Turn the machine heads a little bit at a time while plucking the string and listening to the change in pitch. Tighten the string to raise the pitch. Loosen the string to lower the pitch. Be careful not to accidentally break a string by tightening it too much or too quickly.

The easiest way to tune a guitar is to use an electronic tuner. There are many different kinds available that are fairly inexpensive. You can also download the free online tuner from www.rockhousemethod.com.

Reading a Chord Chart

A chord is a group of notes played together. A chord chart (*chord diagram*) is a graphic representation of part of the fretboard (as if you stood the guitar up from floor to ceiling and looked directly at the front of the neck). The vertical lines represent the strings; the horizontal lines represent the frets.

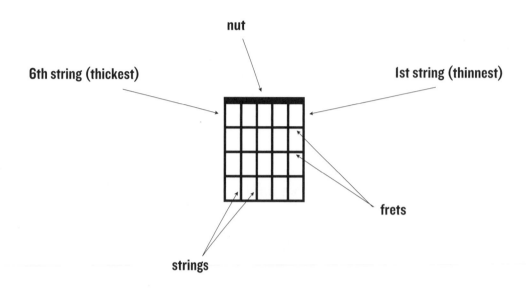

Chord diagrams show which notes to play and which strings they are played on. The solid black dots within the graph represent fretted notes and show you where your fingers should go. Each of these dots will have a number directly below it, underneath the diagram. These numbers indicate which left hand finger to fret the note with (1 = index, 2 = middle, 3 = ring, 4 = pinky). The 0s at the bottom of the diagram show which strings are played open (strummed with no left hand fingers touching them).

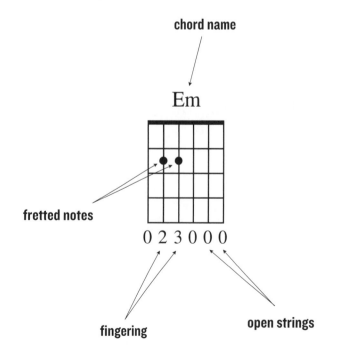

Your First Chords

Our first two chords are two of the easiest and most commonly used chords in rock and blues, A minor and E minor. In the Am chord diagram, the "x" at the 6th string means that string is not played (either muted or not strummed). For each chord, the first photo shows what the chord looks like from the front. The second photo is from the player's perspective. Minor chords are represented in this book using a capital letter, which refers to the letter name of the chord, followed by a lowercase "m" indicating that the chord is a minor chord.

Am

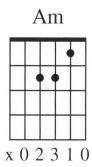

x 0 2 3 1 0

Em

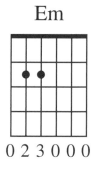

0 2 3 0 0 0

Remember to keep your thumb firmly anchored against the back of the neck. Your fingers should be curled inward toward the fretboard and only the tips of your fingers should be touching the strings. Don't grab the neck with your whole hand; no other parts of your fingers or hand should be touching the neck or any of the other strings. Place your fingertips just to the left of (behind) the fret, pressing the strings inward toward the neck.

Let's start off with a simple downstrum. Fret the Am chord with your left hand. Starting from the 5th string, lightly drag the pick downward across the strings in a smooth motion. Now switch to the Em chord and strum downward from the 6th (thickest) string. The strumming motion should come from your elbow and wrist. When strumming chords, pivot from your elbow and keep your wrist straight. When playing single notes, use more wrist.

One of the hardest things for a beginner to conquer is the ability to play a clean, fully sustained chord without buzzing strings, muted or dead notes. Make sure your left hand is fretting the proper notes and your fingers aren't accidentally touching any of the other strings. Pick each string individually with your right hand, one note at a time. If any of the open strings are deadened or muted, try *slightly* adjusting your fingers. If any of the fretted notes are buzzing, you probably aren't pressing down hard enough with your fingers. It will be difficult at first and might hurt a little, but don't get discouraged. With time and practice, you'll build up callouses on your fingertips. Before you know it, playing chords will be second nature and your fingers will hardly feel it at all.

Strumming Rhythm

Once you have the chords sounding clean and the strumming motion down, the next step is to learn how to change chords quickly and cleanly. Focus on where each finger needs to move for the next chord. Sometimes one or more of your fingers will be able to stay in the same place. Avoid taking your hand completely off the neck. Instead, try to move your whole hand as little as possible and make smaller finger adjustments to change from one chord to the next. When you can change from chord to chord seamlessly, you'll be able to play complete songs.

The following is an example of a *chord progression* and is written on a musical *staff*. A staff is the group of horizontal lines on which music is written. The chord names above the staff show which chord to play, and the *rhythm slashes* indicate the rhythm in which the chords are strummed. In this chord progression, strum each chord twice, using all downstrums. This example also uses *repeat signs* (play through the progression and repeat it again). Listen and play along with the backing track to hear how it should sound. Keep practicing and try to change chords in time without stalling or missing a beat. Count along out loud with each strum, in time and on the beat. Start out slowly if you need to and gradually get it up to speed.

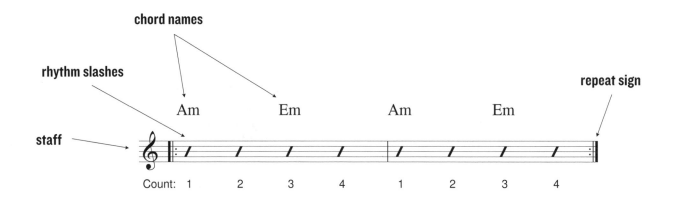

Rhythm Notation

You don't need to read traditional music notation in order to play guitar, but it's helpful to understand a little bit about the concept of rhythm and timing. In most popular rock and blues, music is divided into *measures* of four beats. When a band counts off "One, two, three, four" at the beginning of a song, it represents one complete measure of music. Different types of notes are held for different durations within a measure. For example, a *quarter note* gets one beat because a quarter note is held for one quarter of a measure.

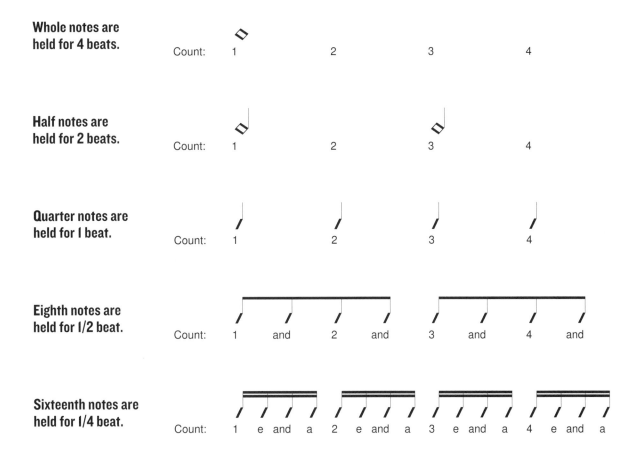

A *tie* is a curved line connecting one note to the next. If two notes are tied, strike only the first one and let it ring out through the duration of the second note (or "tied" note).

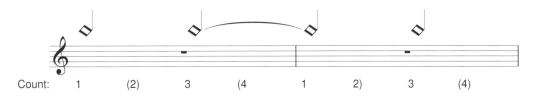

A *dot* after a note increases its value by another 1/2 of its original value. In the following example the half notes are dotted, so they are held for three beats.

Major Open Chords

Now it's time to play some major chords. Major chords have a happy, royal or bright sound, whereas the minor chords have a sad or melancholy type of sound. All of the major and minor chords in this chapter are *open chords* because they contain open strings and are played in the first position on the fretboard. Major chords are represented in this book using a capital letter by itself for the chord name. They can also be shown using the letter name followed by a capital letter M, Maj, or Major. **E**, **A** and **D** are three of the easiest and most used major chords. Many blues songs can be played entirely using just these three chords. The first chord below is the **E** major chord.

E

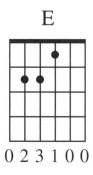

0 2 3 1 0 0

In the **A** chord diagram, the slur going across the notes means you should *barre* (bar) those notes. A barre is executed by placing one finger flat across more than one string. Pick each note of the chord individually to make sure you're applying enough pressure with your finger. Notice that the 6th and 1st strings each have an "x" below them on the diagram, indicating these strings are not played (either muted or not strummed).

A

x 0 1 1 1 x

The last major open chord in this section is the **D** major chord. In this program the 4th and 5th strings are played open; only the 6th string is muted. Another variation of the chord you might encounter will also mute the 5th string. Adding the open 5th string as indicated below gives the chord a fuller sound.

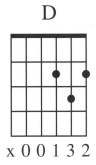

x 0 0 1 3 2

Major Open Chord Strumming Pattern

Here's a progression using the three new chords. This example is played in an eighth note rhythm. Downstrum each chord eight times. Listen to the backing track and practice changing chords cleanly and in time. You can download all of these backing tracks from the website and practice along with them.

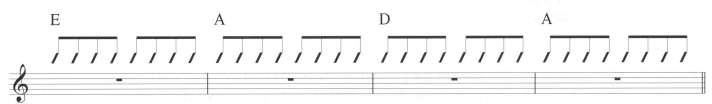

Count: 1 and 2 and 3 and 4 and etc...

Quick Tip!

CHOOSE YOUR TEACHER WISELY

Finding a good guitar teacher is essential, especially for beginners. Playing well and teaching well are separate skills. Just because someone can play guitar doesn't automatically mean they have the proper skills to teach guitar. Before you commit to a teacher, you may want to ask for a trial lesson to make sure you're happy with the communication skills and the teaching method the instructor provides. If you're not learning from someone who knows how to teach, you may have a difficult time.

CHAPTER 2

Tablature Explanation

Tablature (or *tab*) is a number system for reading notes on the neck of a guitar. It does not require you to have knowledge of standard music notation. This system was designed specifically for the guitar. Most music for guitar is available in tab. Tablature is a crucial and essential part of your guitar playing career.

The six lines of the tablature staff represent each of the six strings. The top line is the thinnest (highest pitched) string. The bottom line is the thickest (lowest pitched) string. The lines in between are the 2nd through 5th strings. The numbers placed directly on these lines show you the fret number to play the note at. At the bottom, underneath the staff, is a series of numbers. These numbers show you which left hand fingers you should use to fret the notes.

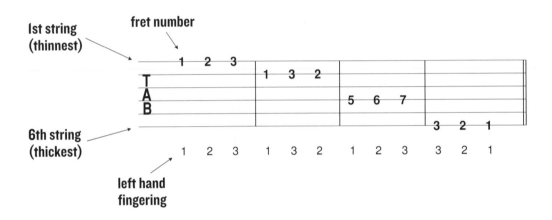

Chords can also be written in tab. If there are several numbers stacked together in a column, those notes should be played or strummed at the same time. Here are the five chords you already know from chapter 1 with the tablature written out underneath each diagram. Since the fingerings are shown on the chord diagrams, we won't bother to repeat them underneath the tab.

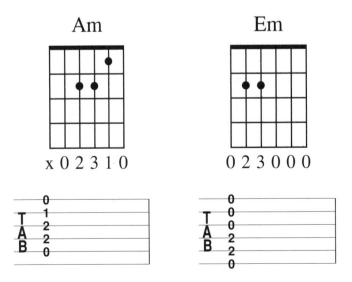

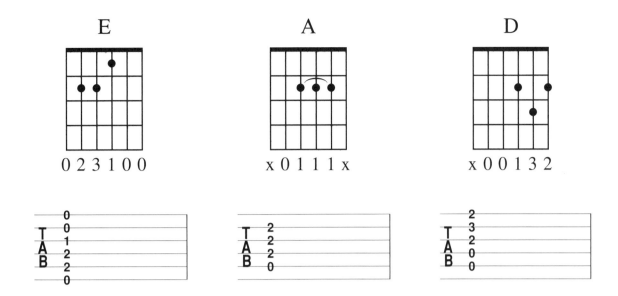

E   A   D

0 2 3 1 0 0   x 0 1 1 1 x   x 0 0 1 3 2

Finger Flexing Exercise

This is a finger exercise in tablature that will build coordination and strengthen your fingers. It's designed to help stretch your hand out, so keep your fingers spread across the first four frets, one finger per fret. Leave your first finger anchored in place and reach for the following three notes by stretching your hand out.

With your right hand, use alternate picking in a consistent down-up-down-up pendulum motion. Alternate picking will help develop speed, smoothness and technique. Practice this exercise using the metronome for timing and control.

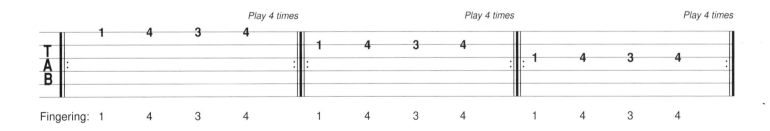

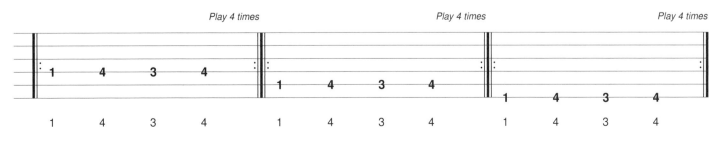

More Major Open Chords

Four more popular major chords are **B**, **C**, **F** and **G**. The hardest one to play is the F chord. This chord is difficult to play because you need to barre the highest two strings with your first finger and put your second and third fingers down straight. If you tilt your first finger barre to the left side, it makes it easier to fret the other notes properly. Pick each note out individually to make sure the chord sounds clean and that you're playing it correctly. You should now know all seven open major chords. Practice playing them and changing from chord to chord efficiently.

B

x x 2 3 4 1

B

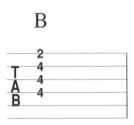

C

C

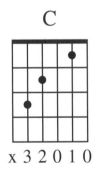

x 3 2 0 1 0

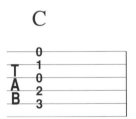

F

x x 3 2 1 1

F

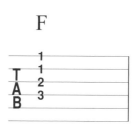

```
    1
    1
T   2
A   3
B
```

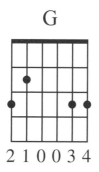

G

2 1 0 0 3 4

G

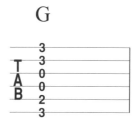

```
    3
    3
T   0
A   0
B   2
    3
```

Quick Tip!

ALWAYS TUNE YOUR GUITAR

Make sure your guitar is in tune every time you play it. You could be playing all of the right notes, but they'll sound incorrect if you haven't tuned up. Even if only one string is slightly out of tune, the simplest of chords will sound bad. It's a good idea to stop and check your tuning from time to time while practicing.

Blues

The following is a basic blues riff in the key of A. This riff is made up of two note chords shown on the tab staff. The chord names above the staff are there as a reference to show you what the basic harmony is while you play along.

This riff should sound very familiar - it's used more than any other blues progression. Plenty of rock and blues classics are played entirely with this one riff repeated over and over. It is made up of 12 measures (or *bars*) of music called the *12-bar blues*, a blues progression consisting of twelve repeated bars of music.

A

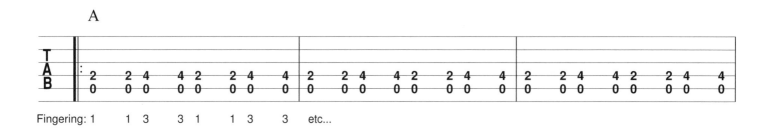

Fingering: 1   1 3   3 1   1 3   3   etc...

D

A   E

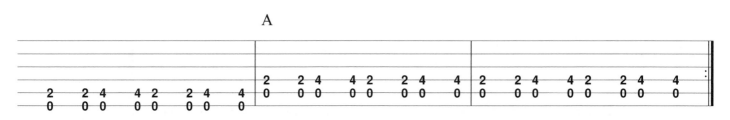

A

Blues is played with a *shuffle feel*, also called a triplet feel. This example was written in eighth notes and the second eighth note of each beat should lag a little. This is referred to as triplet feel because the beat is actually divided by thirds, counted as if there were three eighth notes per beat instead of two. The first part of the beat gets 2/3 of a beat, and the second part only gets 1/3.

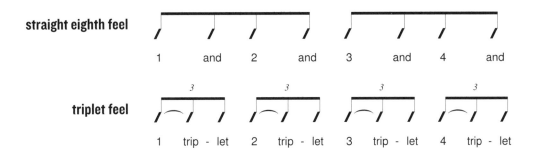

Shuffle feel is a much easier concept to understand by hearing it. Listen to the backing track, count along and try to get the triplet feel in your head. Also, check out almost any blues standard, slow or fast, and you'll probably recognize a shuffle feel being used.

This 12-bar blues riff is also an example of a **I - IV - V** (one - four - five) chord progression. The Roman numerals refer to the steps of the scale, relative to what key the music is in. This blues riff is in the key of A, so the A chord is the **I** chord (also called the *tonic*). The D chord is the **IV** chord (also called the *subdominant*) because in the key of A, D is the fourth step of the scale. Finally, the **V** chord (or *dominant*) is the E chord, because E is the fifth step of the scale in the key of A.

The I - IV - V chord progression is the most common progression used in rock or blues. It's the foundation that all rock and blues was built on and has evolved from. There are many variations, but songs such as "Johnny B. Goode," "You Really Got Me," "Rock and Roll," "I Love Rock and Roll" and "Sympathy for the Devil" are all based on the I - IV - V.

Quick Tip!

TEST YOUR MEMORY

The easiest way to memorize a piece is through repetition. The more you repeat each part, the easier it will be to hear in your head. You may find it easier to memorize something by breaking it into small sections. Be sure to have the first few bits down before moving on and memorization should begin to happen naturally.

More Minor Chords

Now let's play a few more minor chords, **Bm**, **Cm**, and **Dm**. Notice that the Bm and Cm chords both have the exact same fingering. To go from the Bm to the Cm, simply slide your hand up the neck one fret.

Bm

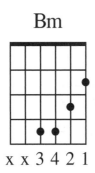

x x 3 4 2 1

Bm

```
      2
      3
T     4
A     4
B
```

Cm

3fr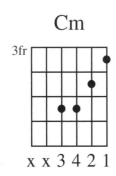

x x 3 4 2 1

Cm

```
      3
      4
T     5
A     5
B
```

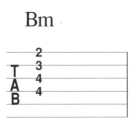

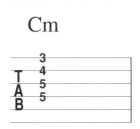

Dm

x 0 0 2 3 1

Dm

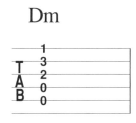

Alternate Strumming

Up until now, we've only been using downstrums. Here's a popular strumming rhythm that combines both up and downstrumming. Play the chords above the staff in the rhythm and strumming pattern indicated. When alternate strumming, keep your arm relaxed and don't grip the pick too tightly. Stay nice and loose so that your strumming sounds smooth, not stiff or forced.

This progression combines both major and minor chords. When changing chords, look for common notes from one chord to the next one; don't move any fingers that can remain on the same notes.

⊓ - downstrum (strum down toward the floor)

∨ - upstrum (strum up toward the ceiling)

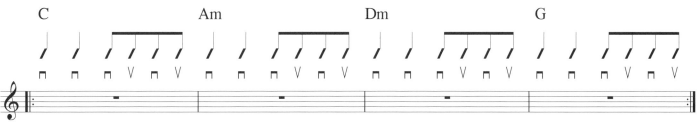

Count: 1   2   3 and 4 and etc...

25

CHAPTER 3

Half Steps & Whole Steps

The distance in pitch between any two musical notes is called an *interval*. An interval is how much higher or lower one note sounds from another, or the space in between the notes. The smallest interval on the guitar is from a fretted note to the fret next to it on the same string. This distance is called a *half step*. Twice the distance, or the distance of two frets, is called a *whole step*.

The musical alphabet uses the letters **A** through **G**. The distance from one letter or note to the next is usually a whole step (two frets), with two exceptions: there is only a half step between the notes **B** and **C** and between the notes **E** and **F**.

whole step	half step	whole step	whole step	half step	whole step	whole step	
A	B	C	D	E	F	G	A

After counting up from **A** to **G**, we get to a higher sounding **A** and can continue to count up higher through the alphabet again from there. The distance from that first **A** to the next **A** (higher or lower) is called an *octave*.

The Chromatic Scale

Counting up or down the musical alphabet in half steps (or frets) is called a chromatic scale. The regular letters of the alphabet are called *natural notes*. Where there is a whole step between two natural notes, the note that falls in between them is a *sharp* (♯) or *flat* (♭) note. The ♯ next to a note makes the note a half step higher. The ♭ lowers the note a half step. For example, the note in between A and B can be called either an A♯ or a B♭ since it's actually the same note with two different names. Whether you call a note sharp or flat depends on what key you're playing in or what the context is. The half steps that occur between B and C and between E and F (where there aren't other notes between them) are referred to as *natural half steps*. If you memorize where these two natural half steps occur you can use that knowledge to find any note on the guitar. Just start with any open string and count up in half steps.

natural half steps

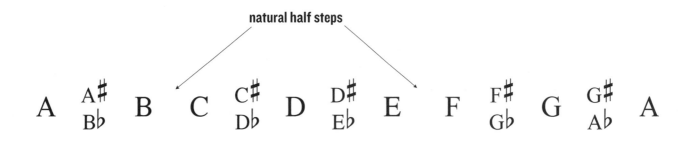

Ascending Chromatic Scale

The following is an exercise that goes up through the chromatic scale in the 1st position of the guitar. Notice that when playing up the scale there are only twelve different notes until you reach an octave and start over with the same letters. These are the twelve notes that make up all music. The name of each note is written above the tab staff.

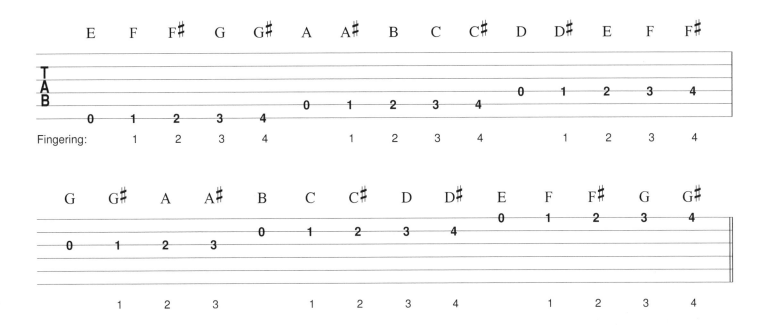

Descending Chromatic Scale

Here's the first position chromatic scale in reverse, descending from highest to lowest note using all flats. Practice both the ascending and descending chromatic scales using the metronome to build up speed and coordination.

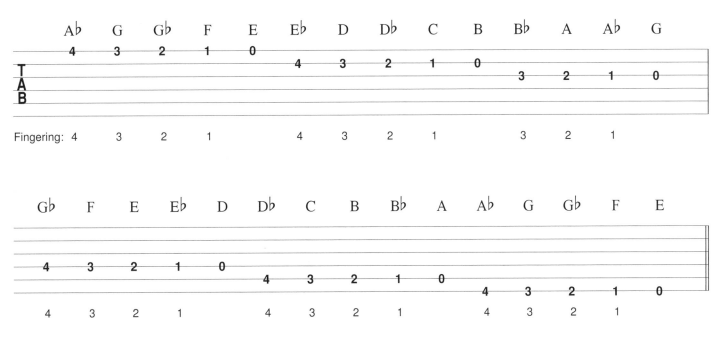

The C Major Scale

The major scale is the foundation of all other scales and chords. If you count up from C to C using only natural notes (C - D - E - F - G - A - B - C) you will have a C major scale. The first note of the scale is C (also known as the *root note*). The root note gives a scale, key or chord its name. For example, the root note of an A chord would be the note A.

Below is the C major scale, starting on the note C at the 8th fret. This is a two octave scale since you can play through two full octaves of the scale in this position. It is also called the *1st position* major scale because the first note played in this position is the root note C. Again, practice this and all scales along with a metronome and always use alternate picking to build up speed and accuracy.

Ascending C Major Scale

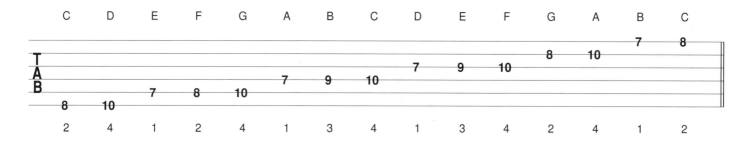

Descending C Major Scale

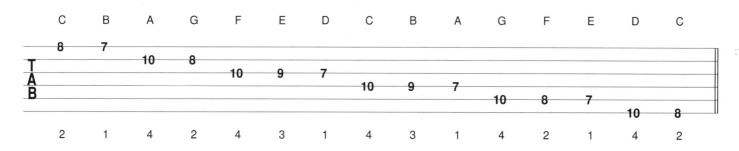

Scale Diagrams

Here is a scale diagram which is similar to the chord diagrams you've seen in chapters 1 and 2. A scale diagram shows you all the notes in the scale within a certain position on the neck. This diagram is for the 1st position C major scale on the previous page. The stacked numbers below indicate the fingering for the notes on each string.

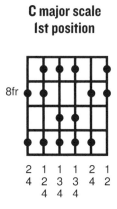

C major scale
Ist position

8fr

```
2 1 1 1 2 1
4 2 3 3 4 2
  4 4 4
```

Intervals of the Major Scale

The sequence of whole steps and half steps is what gives a scale or key its *tonality*. There is a specific sequence of intervals for a major scale and this formula is the same no matter what key the major scale is in. In the chart below, you can see that within the major scale the half steps fall between the 3rd and 4th steps and between the 7th and the octave. All of the other intervals are whole steps. This will be true for any major scale. All together in order, the sequence of intervals (steps) for a major scale are whole - whole - half - whole - whole - whole - half. Scale steps are numbered using roman numerals. The tonic, subdominant, and dominant (I - IV - V) are capitalized because they represent the major chords in the key.

	whole step		whole step		half step		whole step		whole step		whole step		half step	
C		D		E		F		G		A		B		C
I		ii		iii		IV		V		vi		vii		I

Acoustic Rock Chord Progression

The following chord progression is in the key of D major. Notice that it uses the I - IV - V chords of the key in a slightly different order this time. D is the tonic, G is the subdominant and A is the dominant. This is actually a I - V - IV - V progression that's very popular and easy to recognize.

This exercise utilizes a strumming technique that we call a *ghost strum*. A ghost strum occurs when you move the pick over the strings without actually striking them. This allows you to keep your arm moving in a constant down-up-down motion, keeping your playing fluid and in time. The strumming symbols in parentheses indicate where ghost strums occur.

The rhythm used is an example of *syncopation*. You're playing a syncopated rhythm if there's one or more strums off the beat, or on the upbeat instead of the downbeat. The strum on beat 2 1/2 is tied to beat 3, so you don't strum directly on beat 3.

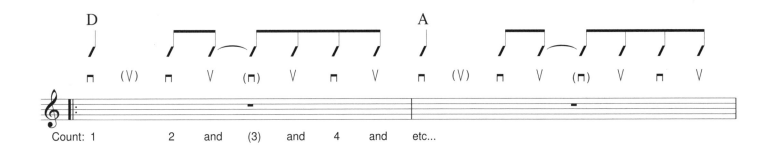

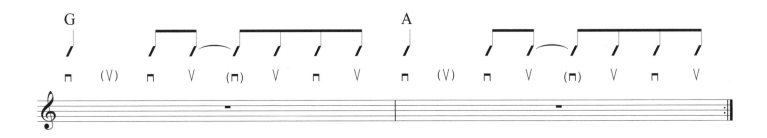

If you're having trouble changing from chord to chord smoothly, isolate the change and just practice going back and forth between those two chords. With practice, you'll build finger memory and your fingers will instinctively know where to go. Play this rhythm along with the backing track and get the changes, the feel and the strumming motion down.

Making Melodies

Now it's time to start creating some melodies and leads. Let's take the C major scale you just learned and move the entire pattern up one whole step (two frets), so that your second finger is at the 10th fret on the note D. If you play the exact same pattern from there, you will have a D major scale. This is called *transposing* the scale.

D major scale
1st position

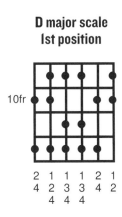

The D Major Scale

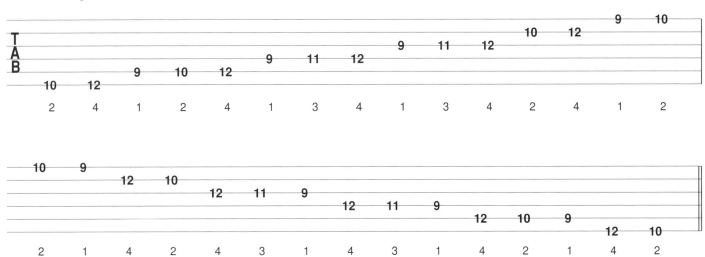

Remember that the key of C major is the only key made up of all natural notes. When the major scale is transposed to a different key, *accidentals* (sharps or flats) need to be added to some of the notes. This is to make sure that all of the whole steps and half steps are between the proper steps of the scale. For example, if you start on D (the root note), the second note of the scale is E and the third note is an F. In the major scale formula, there has to be a whole step between the 2nd and 3rd steps. Since there is a *natural half step* between E and F, you need to add a sharp to the F to make it a whole step up from E. The C also needs to be sharped to have a whole step between the 6th and 7th steps. The key of D major contains two sharps.

whole step	whole step	half step	whole step	whole step	whole step	half step	
D	E	F♯	G	A	B	C♯	D
I	ii	iii	IV	V	vi	vii	I

Improvising

You can play the D major scale along with the Acoustic Rock Chord Progression from the previous lesson and start to learn how to play solos. Play along with the backing track and experiment with the notes to create your own little melodies. You can start by playing up or down the scale, then mix it up a little. Play small parts of the scale in sections, hold some notes out longer than others and try to ascend or descend a few notes at a time. Avoid just playing the entire two octave scale all at once; you only need to use a few notes to come up with the most memorable and tasteful melodies. Keep it simple, follow your ear and listen for which notes sound good to you and in what order. Use your instinct and let your creative side come out.

Here is an example of some melodies you can play. For your reference, the chord names are located above the staff. On the DVD that follows along with this book, note that these melodies were improvised during the lesson as an example. This solo has been tabbed out here to get you started and show you how it's done. The point of this lesson is for you to understand how to improvise, so don't get caught up in trying to learn this example note for note. Instead, take a quick look through these riffs and then spend more time creating your own.

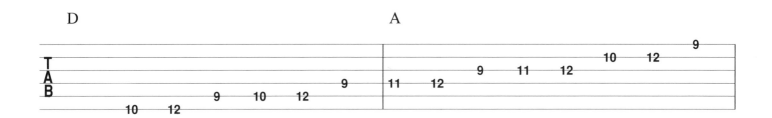

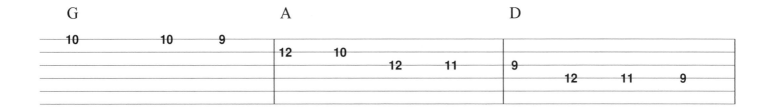

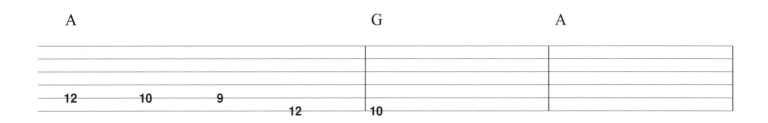

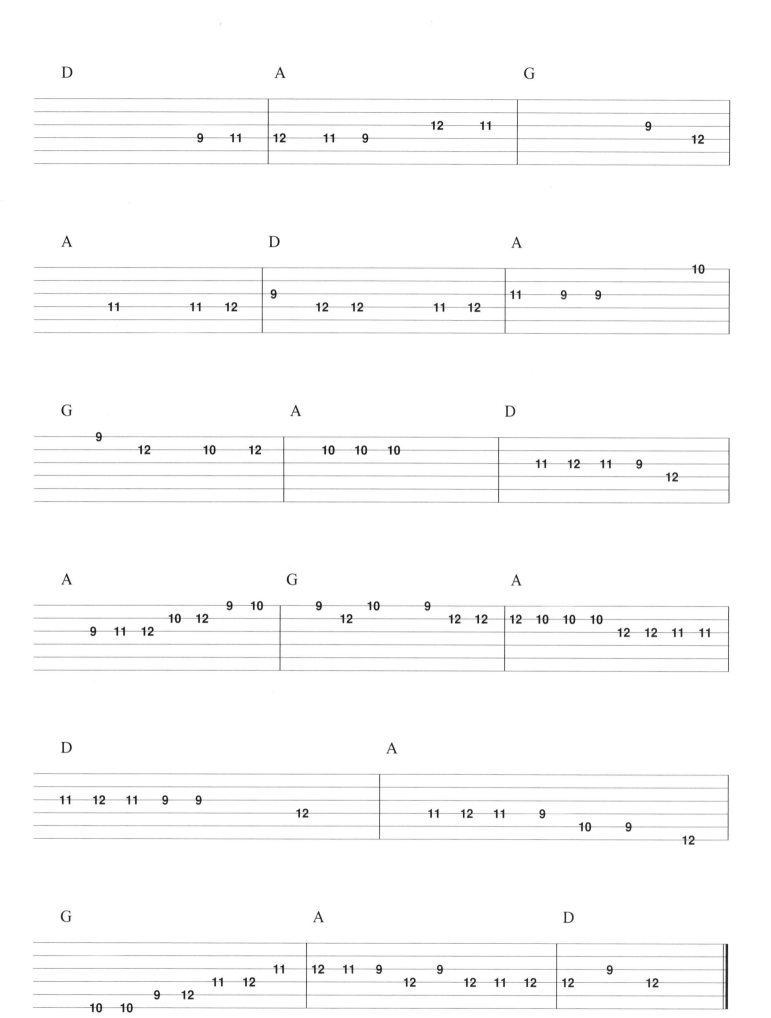

House of Blues is the Home of Live Entertainment.

Have an intimate yet high energy experience at one of our many venues across the country.

CHAPTER 4
Alternate Picking

Let's start this section with an alternate picking exercise to help coordinate your right hand. Instead of strumming the chords, you might pick the notes of a chord out individually and let them ring out together.

Fret an open D chord and hold the chord shape with your left hand while picking out the individual notes in the order notated on the tab staff. This picking pattern (indicated by which number string you pick) is 4 - 1 - 3 - 1 - 2 - 1. Recite the string number while you pick each one to help memorize the order. Use a down-up-down-up alternate picking pattern. Notice that the 1st string is always uppicked, while the other strings are all downpicked. Try to hold one of your right hand fingers on the body of the guitar to help give you added support and control. Practice playing in a steady, even rhythm, in time with a metronome.

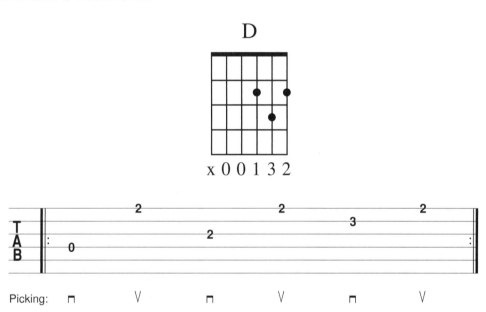

You can use this pattern for the other chords too. Here's the same pattern with a C chord.
Once you get the alternate picking motion down, get creative and come up with your own patterns.

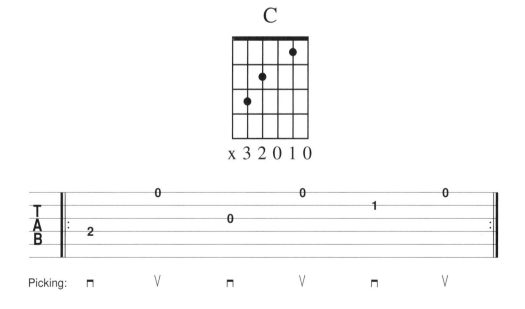

Essential Acoustic Chords

Major and Minor Barre Chords

Two very important chords are the F and B♭ barre chords. These are full barre chords containing no open strings, so they are *moveable* chords. You can transpose them to any fret.

Full barre chords are especially difficult to play. For the F barre chord, you need to barre your first finger across all six strings, then add the other three notes as well. Pick out each note individually to make sure it sounds clean and you've got it down. After mastering these chords, you'll be able to play in any key and position on the guitar.

1 3 4 2 1 1

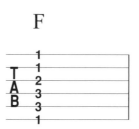

Notice that the lowest note of the chord is the root note. Using the musical alphabet and the chromatic scale from Chapter 3, you can move full barre chords up the neck and change them to any chord in the scale. Use the following chart to find any chord along the 6th string by moving the F chord.

6th string notes (F chord)	E	F	F♯	G	G♯	A	A♯	B	C	C♯	D	D♯	E
fret number	Open	1	2	3	4	5	6	7	8	9	10	11	12
5th string notes (B♭ chord)	A	B♭	B	C	C♯	D	D♯	E	F	F♯	G	G♯	A

For the B♭ chord, you need to barre across three strings with your third finger. The Fm and B♭m chords are only slightly different. All of these chords are also moveable using the chart.

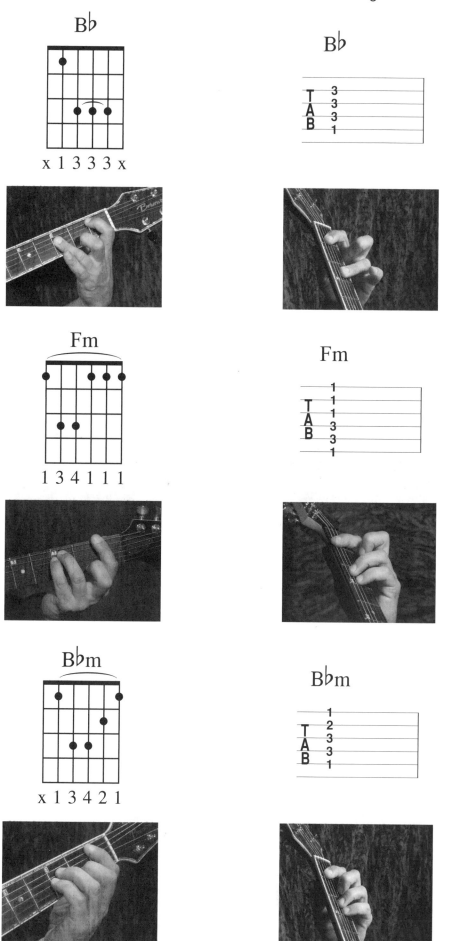

Major 7th and Minor 7th Barre Chords

Now let's move on to the major 7th (maj7) and minor 7th (m7) barre chords, which are also all moveable. The 7th chords are *extensions* of the original major and minor chords - they add a new note to the chord which gives it more flavor and a jazzier sound.

For the **Gmaj7** chord, you need to mute or deaden the 5th string with your fretting hand. If you tilt your first finger down slightly, it will lightly touch the 5th string and mute it. The **Cmaj7** chord doesn't use a barre, which makes it slightly easier to play. In both chords, the 1st string is not strummed.

Gmaj7

1 x 3 4 2 x

Gmaj7

```
   3
T  4
A  4
B
   3
```

Cmaj7

3fr

x 1 3 2 4 x

Cmaj7

```
   5
T  4
A  5
B  3
```

From the minor barre chords you've just learned, all you need to do is lift your pinky off either chord and you'll have the minor 7th chords: **Fm7** and **B♭m7**.

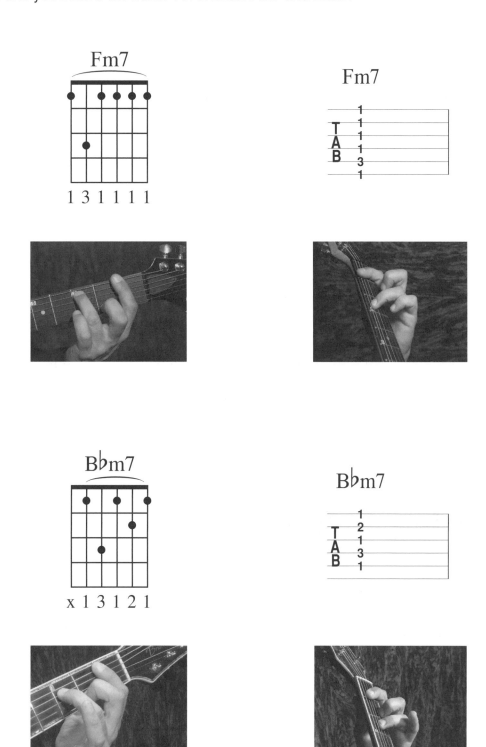

Memorize and practice all of the moveable barre chords. Make sure you have them down perfectly and can play them cleanly because we'll be using them in the upcoming sections. All of these chords are essential for playing rock and blues.

Arpeggio Chord Progression

An arpeggio is defined as the notes of a chord played separately. In this exercise, fret a C major chord and pick the notes separately in their order on the tab staff. Next, change to the Em chord. Here you can use a slightly different fingering for the Em that will make it easier to change chords. Just leave your second finger in the same place for both chords. The left hand fingering is notated under the tab staff. Pick the notes in the sequence indicated while holding down the chord fingering, allowing the notes to ring out.

This is a common pattern used in ballads and slow tempo songs. Listen to the backing track and play along. Notice the timing is different than the regular 4/4 (four beats per measure) we've been playing up until now. This rhythm only contains three quarter notes per measure, counted: "One, two, three, one, two, three." A waltz is a good example of 3/4 time. The picking pattern here is also different. Instead of alternate picking, downpick the lower strings in a row, then uppick the higher strings.

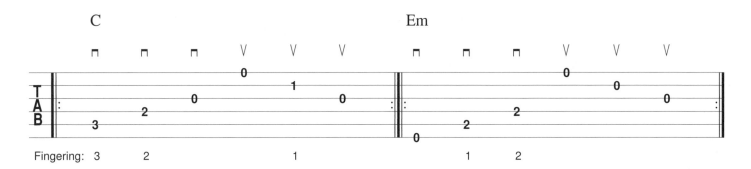

Changing the Feel of a Song

By altering the strumming or picking pattern of a chord progression, you can dramatically change the style. In this section, we'll show you how to take a simple chord change and use it to play many different genres of music, all against the same bass and drum backing track. This demonstrates the power of the guitar and its ability to dictate the feel of the song.

A Cadd9 chord (or a Csus2 chord) is a slight variation of the regular C chord. Notice how similar the fingering is to the G chord and how easy it is to switch back and forth between them. Just leave your third and fourth fingers stationary and move your first and second fingers up or down one string.

G

2 1 0 0 3 4

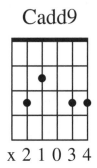

Cadd9

x 2 1 0 3 4

Rock

This is a standard rock rhythm you've already played using the new progression.

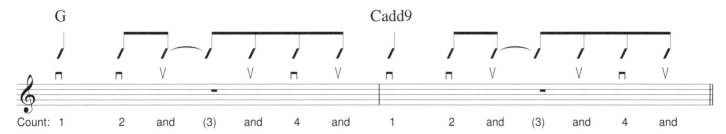

Reggae

Reggae uses all upstrokes. Following each upstrum of the pick, mute the strings with your picking hand in time and on the downbeat to give it that reggae feel.

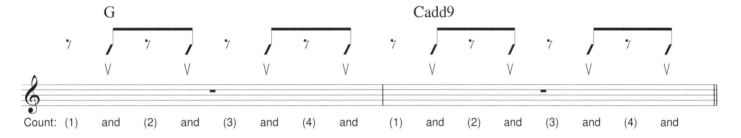

Ballad

Here's another rock ballad pattern. Use the same picking technique from the previous lesson, downpicking the first half of the measure and uppicking the second half.

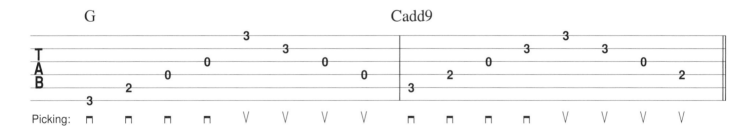

Country

Country guitar rhythms alternate between picking and strumming. Pick the lower notes on the downbeats, and follow the picked notes with regular strums on the upbeats.

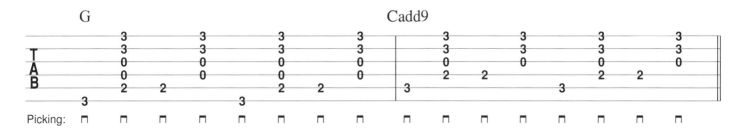

CHAPTER 5
Fingerpicking

When applying the fingerpicking technique to the guitar, use only your fingers to play the notes and chords; no pick is used. Pluck downward with your thumb and upward with your fingers. Thumb and fingers are labeled as *p* (thumb), *i* (index), *m* (middle), *a* (ring finger). These are international fingerpicking symbols.

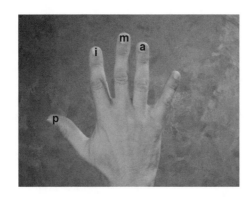

In the following exercise, fret and hold the chord (D, Cadd9 or G) and pick out the notes in their order on the tab staff. Use the letters underneath to show you which right hand fingers to use. There are also many hybrid ways to fingerpick; for example using your pick, but also incorporating some of your fingers to pluck the strings. Once you have this technique down, have fun experimenting with it.

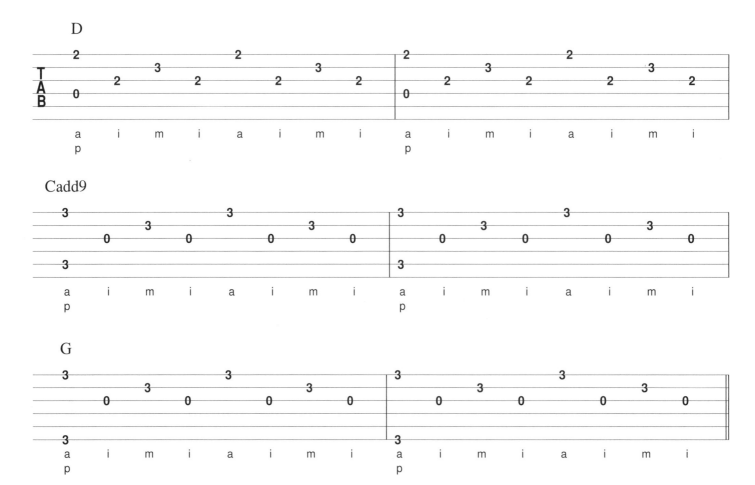

Major Seventh Chord Progression

Now let's take the major seventh chords from the last chapter and play them at the 5th fret: Amaj7 and Dmaj7. The rhythm for this progression is syncopated, so use the same basic ghost strumming technique you learned earlier to help keep a smooth, pendulum motion with your right arm. Practice this progression along with the backing track that's available on the CD and the Lesson Support Site.

Amaj7
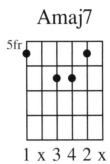
1 x 3 4 2 x

Dmaj7
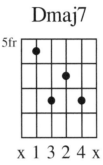
x 1 3 2 4 x

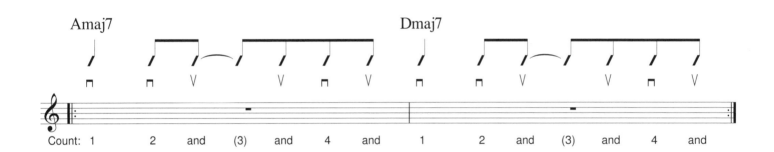

Quick Tip!

LEARN GRADUALLY AND HAVE REALISTIC GOALS

Don't try to play a lot of things you aren't ready for. Be realistic about your capabilities as a beginner and learn gradually. If you progress at a steady, methodical rate, your technique and control of the guitar will become solid as you advance. Strive to master each new technique, chord or scale before moving on to something else. Attempting things that you're not quite ready for can discourage you instead of inspire you to play.

The Minor Pentatonic Scale

Minor pentatonic scales are the most commonly used scales for playing rock and blues solos. The pentatonic is a five note scale, or an abbreviated version of the full natural minor scale. The word "pentatonic" comes from the greek words, "penta" (five) and "tonic" (the keynote).

Memorize and practice this scale; it's the one you'll use most often for playing melodies and leads. There are five different positions of this scale, each beginning on a different note of the scale. All five positions are shown here in tab. To the right of each tab staff is a scale diagram. These are similar to the chord diagrams we've previously used. A scale diagram shows you all the notes in the scale within a certain position on the neck. The stacked numbers below the diagram indicate the fingering for the notes on each string.

1st Position A Minor Pentatonic Scale

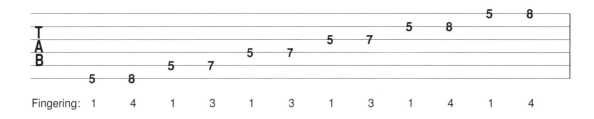

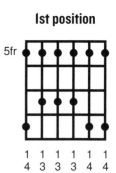

2nd Position A Minor Pentatonic Scale

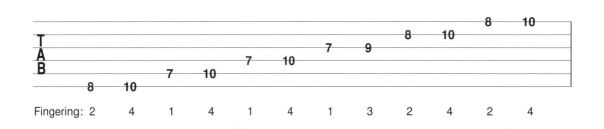

3rd Position A Minor Pentatonic Scale

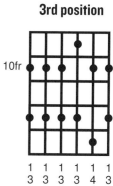

3rd position

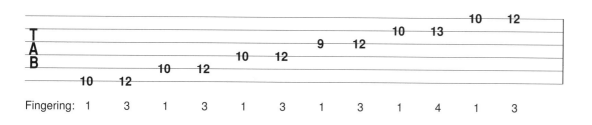

Fingering: 1   3   1   3   1   3   1   3   1   4   1   3

4th Position A Minor Pentatonic Scale

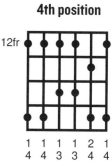

4th position

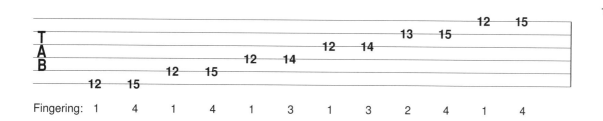

Fingering: 1   4   1   4   1   3   1   3   2   4   1   4

5th Position A Minor Pentatonic Scale

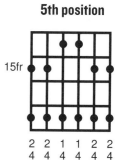

5th position

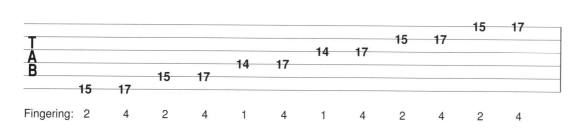

Fingering: 2   4   2   4   1   4   1   4   2   4   2   4

The Minor Pentatonic Scale Fretboard Diagram

Once you have all five positions of the minor pentatonic scales mastered, you'll be able to play solos in any position on the neck. Remember that there are only five different name notes in the scale, and the different positions are just groupings of these same notes in different octaves and different places on the neck. The 4th and 5th positions from the previous page can be transposed one octave lower (shown below in the fretboard diagram). Notice how each position overlaps the next; the left side of one position is the right side of the next one and so on. Think of these scale positions as building blocks (like Legos). When soloing, you can move from position to position and play across the entire fretboard.

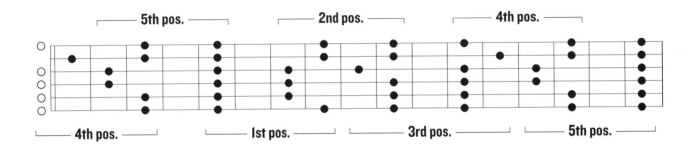

Quick Tip!

DEVELOP GOOD PRACTICE HABITS

Knowing how to practice efficiently will accelerate your progress. Set aside a certain amount of time for practicing and have a routine that reviews all of the techniques you know. Create your own exercises that target weaknesses in your playing. It's important to experiment and get creative as well; try things fast or slow, light or hard, soft or loud.

Triplet Lead Pattern

Here is the A minor pentatonic scale you've just learned played in groups of three notes, or triplets. Count "one - two - three, one - two - three" out loud while you play through this exercise to get the triplet feel in your head. This is a standard lead pattern exercise, designed to help you build coordination and learn how to begin using the minor pentatonics for playing leads. Use alternate picking and the metronome to start out slowly and get the rhythm. Gradually speed it up and before you know it, you'll be playing blazing rock and blues guitar solos.

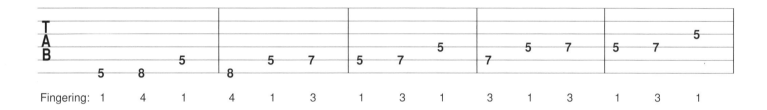

Fingering:

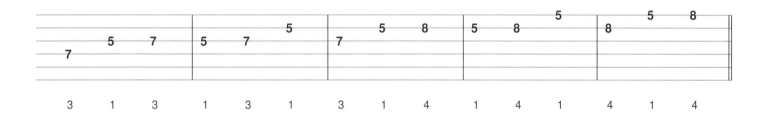

Now let's play the same pattern in reverse, back down the scale in triplets. After you have the pattern memorized, use it to play the 2nd position minor pentatonic, as well as the other three positions available on our lesson support website. You can also use this pattern to practice any other scales you've learned.

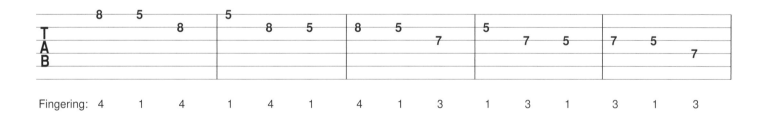

Fingering:

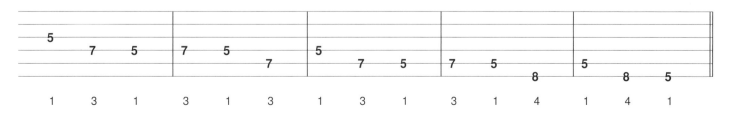

Acoustic Rock Rhythm

Here's a popular acoustic rock rhythm using all barre chords. Play along to the backing track and get the quick strumming feel down. You can take all of the chords you've learned and play them in this or any other rhythm, then try writing some of your own songs.

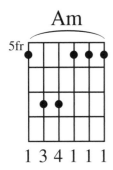
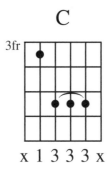

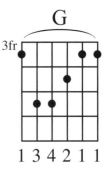

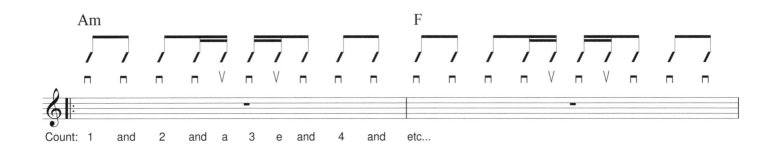

Count: 1   and   2   and   a   3   e   and   4   and   etc...

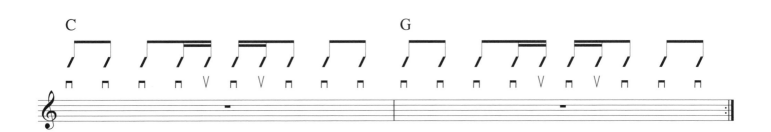

end of chapter 5

Congratulations! You've just completed all of the lessons on CD disc 1. The backing tracks for many of these lessons are included in the Music Minus One Backing Tracks at the end of each disc for you to practice along with. Before you continue to the next section, use your member number and log on to www.rockhousemethod.com to visit our online community. Review the additional information, take a quiz and test your knowledge. See you in the next section!

CHAPTER 6
Using the Capo

A capo (pronounced *kay-po*) is an accessory used to instantly transpose the entire guitar. There are different types of capos available ranging from clamp capos (shown below) to capos with an elastic material that wraps around the neck to keep it in place. A capo essentially barres across all six strings of the guitar, transposing all of the open strings up to the fret where the capo is placed. The capo can be used like a moveable nut; wherever the capo is placed becomes the new open position. All of the open chords can be played relative to the capo, which automatically transposes them to the new key. A capo is a very versatile and inexpensive accessory.

The photos below show a clamp capo being properly placed at the 2nd fret. Capos are popular at the 1st, 2nd, 3rd, 5th and 7th frets, but you can place a capo anywhere at all on the neck. A capo at the 12th fret transposes the guitar one octave higher and gives it a bright, mandolin tone. When there are multiple guitars playing at the same time, it's common to have one or more guitars capoed at different frets. This helps to create a fuller sound by having individual guitars playing the same progression transposed to different keys and different places on the neck.

Placing a clamp capo on the neck.

A capo properly placed at the 2nd fret.

Generally, capoed guitar parts are shown in tab relative to the placement of the capo. The music will be transposed to show the part as it would normally be shown in open position. The zeros in the tab are actually the fret that the capo is placed at. Try the following D major progression below, then place the capo at the 5th fret and play the same progression. The progression has now been transposed up to G major, and although you're still fingering D, G, and A chords, the actual sounding chords would be G, C and D. By placing the capo at the 7th fret, the progression will be transposed up to A major and the actual sounding chords will be A, D and E.

D   G   A

⊓   ⊓ V   V ⊓ V   etc.

```
   |-----2---2--2-----2---2--2-|---3---3-3----3---3-3---|-------------------------|--------------------------|
 T |-----3---3--3-----3---3--3-|---3---3-3----3---3-3---|---2---2-2----2---2-2----|----2---2-2-----2---2-2---|
 A |:----2---2--2-----2---2--2-|---0---0-0----0---0-0---|---2---2-2----2---2-2----|----2---2-2-----2---2-2--:|
 B |-----0---0--0-----0---0--0-|---0---0-0----0---0-0---|---2---2-2----2---2-2----|----2---2-2-----2---2-2---|
   |-----0---0--0-----0---0--0-|---2---2-2----2---2-2---|---0---0-0----0---0-0----|----0---0-0-----0---0-0---|
   |---------------------------|---3---3-3----3---3-3---|-------------------------|--------------------------|
```

Open E Tuning

Open tuning refers to the act of tuning all of the strings on the guitar to the notes of a chord. Although this makes playing leads and scales pretty difficult, open tuning opens up new possibilites for playing rhythms and chord progressions. Since the entire guitar is tuned to a chord in open tuning, you can play barre chords by using just one finger barred across all six strings. This frees up your other fingers to easily play suspensions and variations.

For open E tuning, start out in standard tuning and tune the 5th string up to B, the 4th string up to E, and the 1st string up to G#. Now the open string notes will be E - B↑ - E↑ - G#↑ - B - E (all of the notes in an E major chord). The arrows are there to show you which direction to tune the string if you're starting out from standard tuning.

Open E Tuning Rhythm

The staff below shows a simple progression you can play in open E tuning. It incorporates dead strums and the three chords E, G and A. You can barre across all six strings for the G and A chords using your third finger or your first and third fingers. Experiment with playing chords in open E tuning and decide which is most comfortable for you.

Open tuning also works great in combination with a capo or a slide. Here are a few more open tunings you can experiment with.

Open G tuning: D↓ - G↓ - D - G - B - D↓

Open D tuning: D↓ - A - D - F#↓ - A↓ - D↓

Open E5 tuning #1: E - B↑ - E↑ - B↑ - B - E

Open E5 tuning #2: E - E↓ - E↑ - B↑ - B - B↓

Fingerpicking Pattern

Let's begin this section with a quick review of the fingerpicking technique and notation symbols from Chapter 5. When applying the fingerpicking technique to the guitar, pluck downward with your thumb and upward with your fingers. Thumb and fingers are labeled as *p* (thumb), *i* (index), *m* (middle), *a* (ring finger).

In the following exercise, fret and hold each chord and pick out the notes in the order shown on the tab staff. Use the letters underneath to show you which right hand fingers to use. As you get comfortable with the fingerpicking technique, try combining it with a capo and some of the open tunings from the previous lesson.

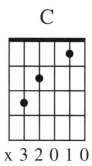 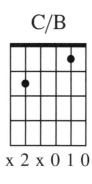 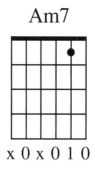

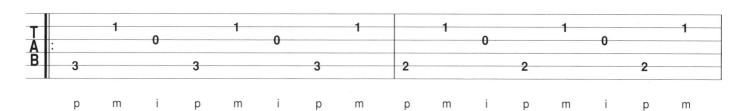

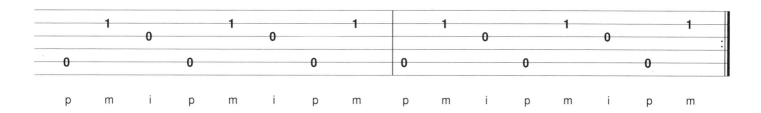

Acoustic Slapping

While playing fingerstyle (without a pick), you can add a percussive, rhythmic feel to a chord progression by slapping the strings with your thumb. In the exercise below, fret the G chord in the first measure and follow the p-i-m-a right hand fingering, paying attention to where the rhythmic slaps occur in the progression.

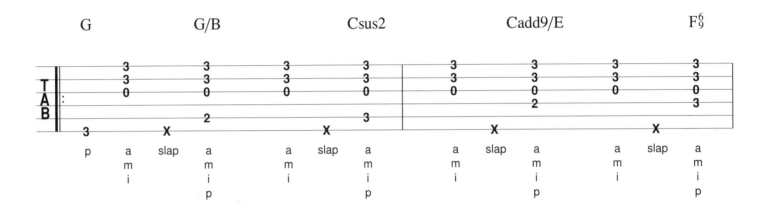

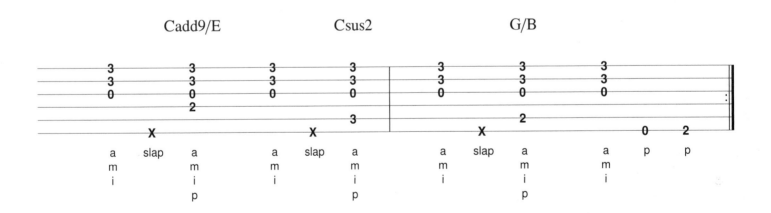

CHAPTER 7
House of the Rising Sun

Now it's time to have some fun! Here's a popular standard for acoustic guitar using all basic open chords. The timing (or *meter*) for this song is in three and can be counted as 3/4 or 6/8 time. Listen to the CD track to get a feel for the rhythm. Memorize the strumming pattern indicated above the first measure and use this pattern throughout the song. Keep your strumming arm loose and relaxed and make sure you change chords smoothly and efficiently. The key of the song is A minor, so you can also have fun playing your own solos over the progression using the A minor pentatonic scales we've used in the previous lessons.

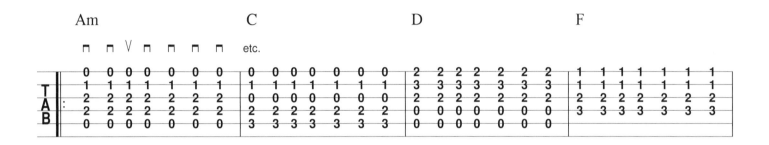

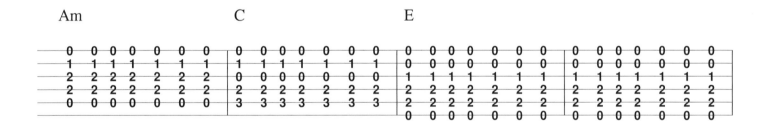

Natural Minor Scales

Many modern Rock and Blues players have incorporated the use of full natural minor scales into their soloing. The pentatonic scales you've already learned are abbreviated versions of the regular major and minor scales. The pentatonic scales contain five notes; the natural minor scale contains seven notes. The word "natural" refers to the fact that the scale is in its original unaltered state. The natural minor scale can be used to create more complex and interesting melodies.

Below are the five basic positions of the B natural minor scale shown ascending and descending. The root notes have all been circled on the staff and scale diagrams.

1st Position B Minor Scale

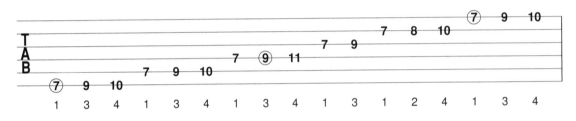

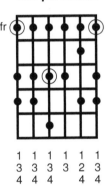

1st position

2nd Position B Minor Scale

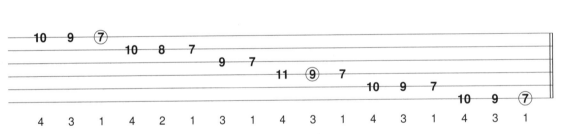

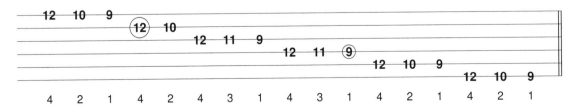

2nd position

3rd Position B Minor Scale

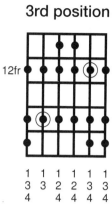

3rd position

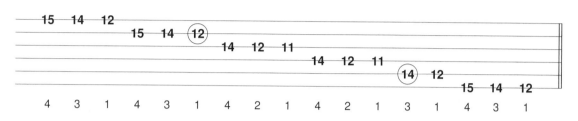

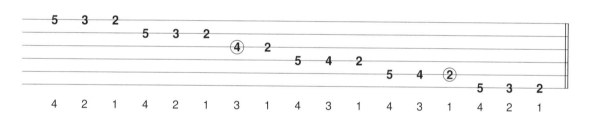

4th Position B Minor Scale

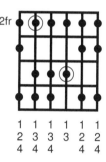

4th position

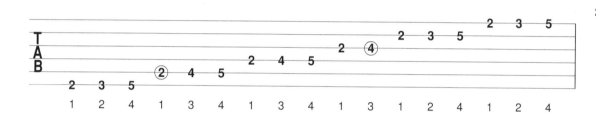

5th Position B Minor Scale

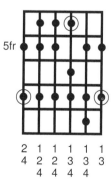

5th position

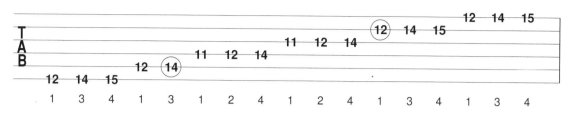

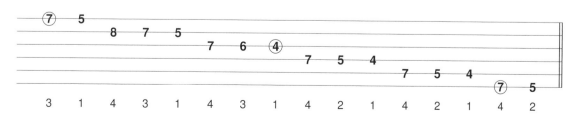

Minor Seventh Rhythm

In this lesson, we'll introduce some new chords and show you a progression in the key of B minor. Once you've got the rhythm down, you can try soloing over the rhythm track using all of the B natural minor scale positions.

These minor seventh chords have slightly different fingerings from the ones you've already learned. For the Bm7 chord, deaden the 5th string by slightly tilting the second finger on your left hand to mute the string. Use the same technique while playing the Em7 chord to mute the 4th string with your first finger. Pay close attention to the DVD lesson for important tips.

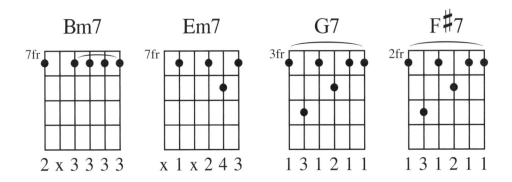

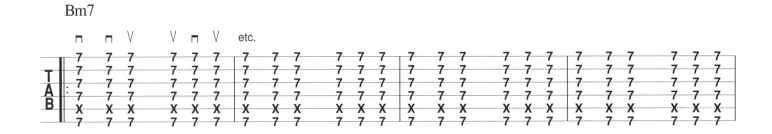

The following improvised lead example from the DVD has been transcribed in tab for your reference. The audio is also included on the accompanying CD at regular and slow speeds. Play through the riffs to get some ideas on how to use the B natural minor scales and all of the lead techniques to create your own melodic solos in minor keys.

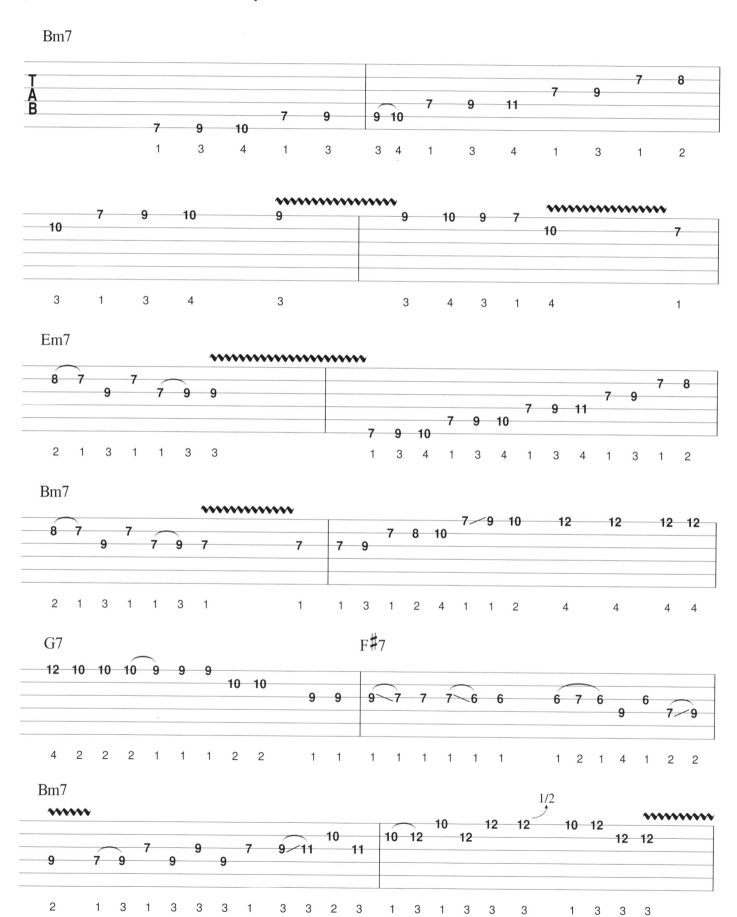

Bm7

Em7

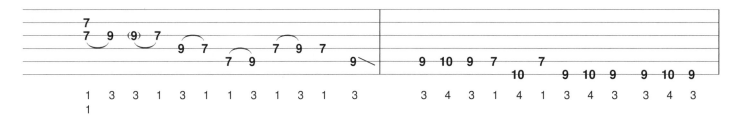

Bm7

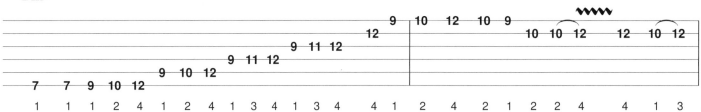

G7

F♯7

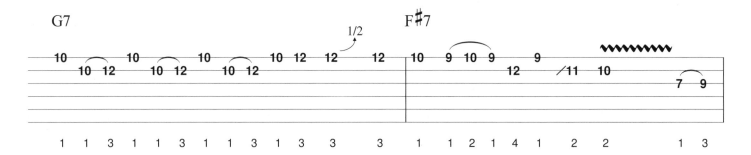

Bm7

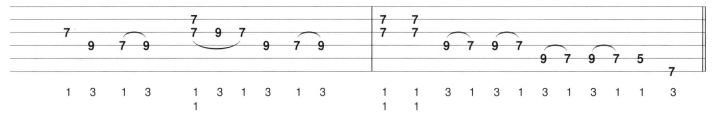

Come visit us at one of our House of Blues Club venues where you can enjoy southern-inspired cuisine in our restaurant.

Experience an intimate fine dining, entertainment and lounge experience at the House of Blues Foundation Room.

CHAPTER 8
Major Scale Triplet Lead Pattern

1st Position Triplet Lead Pattern

Here is the 1st position C major scale played in groups of three notes, or triplets. This pattern is similar to the triplet lead pattern we used for the minor pentatonic scales. Play through the scale in groups of three notes, with each group of three beginning on the next successive scale degree. Each measure below contains one triplet for reading convenience. Practice along with a metronome and keep the timing even and steady. Count "one - two - three, one - two - three" or "one trip-let, two trip-let" out loud to get the triplet feel in your head.

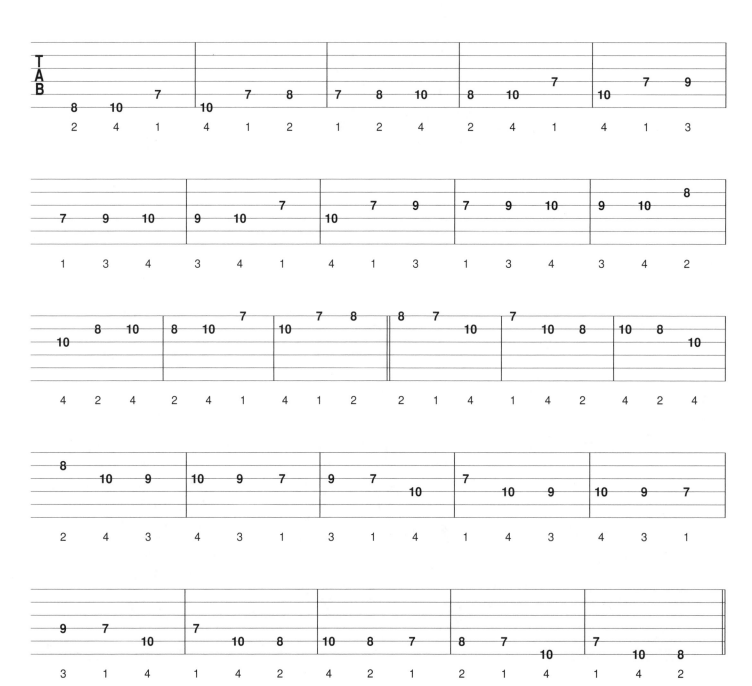

2nd Position Triplet Lead Pattern

The purpose of playing these lead patterns is for you to get used to phrasing the scales in many different ways, instead of just playing them forwards and backwards. If you think of the scales and chords as your alphabet and vocabulary, then practicing lead patterns is similar to honing your writing or typing skills.The more control you have over scale patterns, the easier it will be for you to play creative and interesting melodies. Below is the 2nd position of the major scale triplet pattern. After you've learned this one, play the remaining three positions using this pattern.

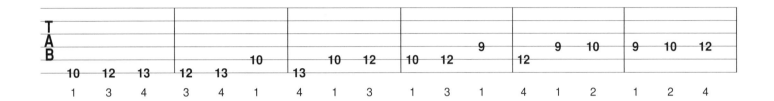

System 1 fingering: 1 3 4 3 4 1 4 1 3 1 3 1 4 1 2 1 2 4

System 2 fingering: 2 4 1 4 1 2 1 1 3 1 3 1 3 1 3 1 3 4

System 3 fingering: 3 4 1 4 1 3 1 3 4 4 3 1 3 1 4 1 4 3

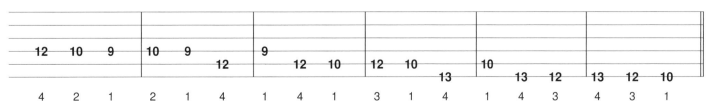

System 4 fingering: 4 3 1 3 1 3 1 3 1 3 1 1 2 1 4 1 4 2

System 5 fingering: 4 2 1 2 1 4 1 4 1 3 1 4 1 4 3 4 3 1

Playing the Major Scale Over a Blues Progression

The backing track for this example is a slow blues that you can solo over using the C major scales. Play through this improvised example solo and follow along with the DVD and CD to get some ideas for creating melodic solos using the full major scale in all five positions.

This slow blues is in 6/8 time, a common time signature for this genre. It can be counted in groups of three, a triplet for each downbeat (one-two-three, one-two-three). The use of sycopation for many of the riffs gives the lead a spontaneous and soulful style.

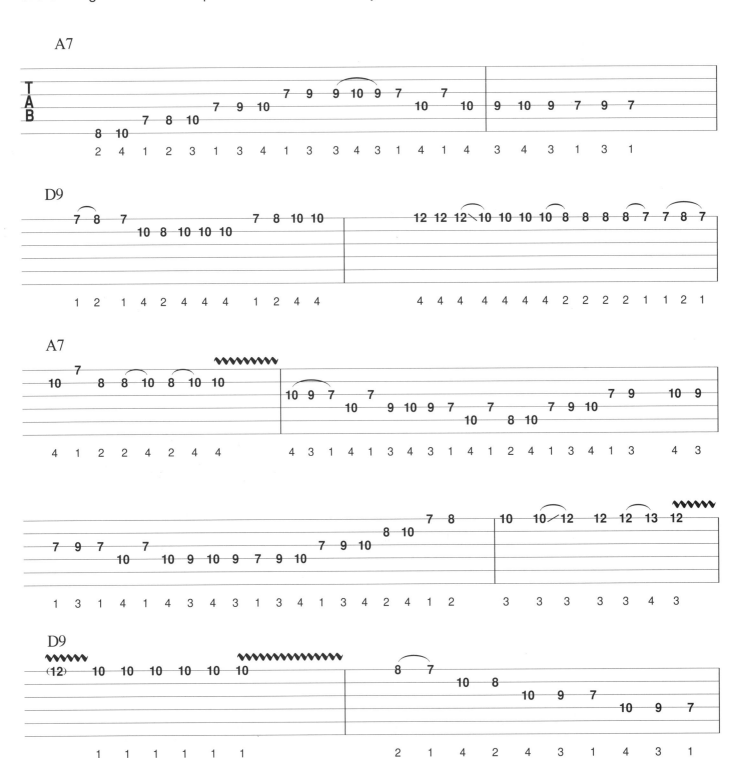

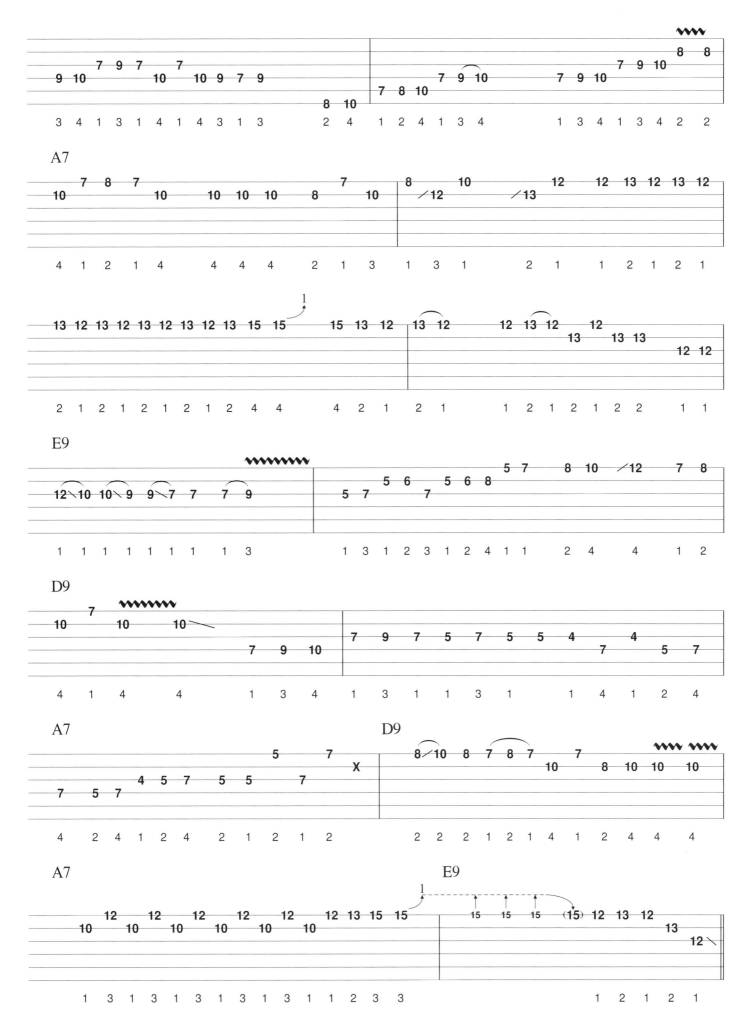

Sixteenth Note Scale Pattern

The final lesson in this program introduces a new scale pattern designed to help build coordination and diversify your phrasing when using the major and minor scales.

Sixteenth Note C Major Scale Pattern

Sixteenth notes are four notes played within one beat. Sixteenth notes can be counted as groups of four notes: "one, two, three, four, one, two, three, four." You can also count sixteenth notes as "one-e-and-a, two-e-and-a," to help keep track of what number beat you are on. The following sixteenth note scale pattern ascends and descends through the 1st position of the C major scale in groups of four notes; the barlines have been placed after each grouping for reading convenience and the left hand fingering is indicated below the tab staff. Practice slowly with a metronome and gradually build up speed, remembering to use consistent, alternate picking. Once you've got the phrasing down, try playing all five positions of the major scale using this pattern.

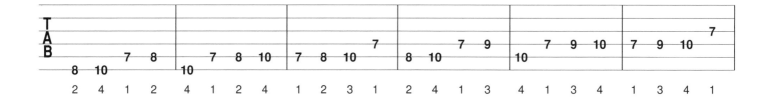

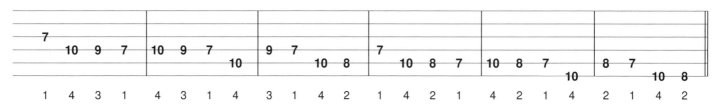

Sixteenth Note B Minor Scale Pattern

Now let's take that sixteenth note pattern and use it to play the 1st position B natural minor scale. Watch your left hand fingering and make sure you use alternate picking to build speed and keep your timing steady and smooth. When you've got it down using the 1st positon, transpose the pattern to all of the remaing positions of the natural minor scale.

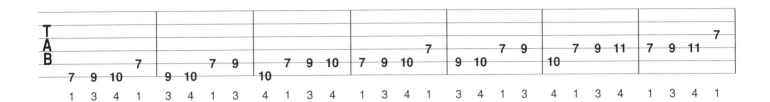

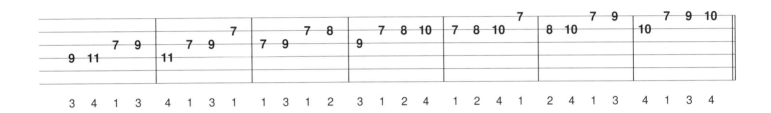

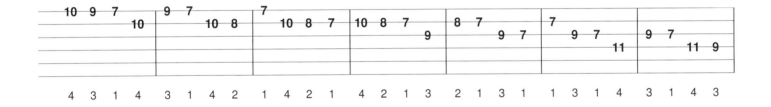

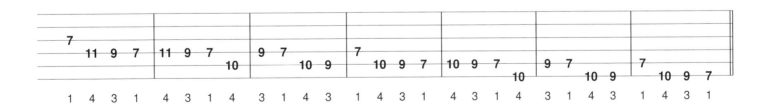

end of chapter 8

Congratulations! You've just completed all of the lessons on CD disc 2. By using your lifetime membership to the Lesson Support Site, you can continue to progress as a guitarist and utilize the limitless resources avialable there. Network with other musicians, post your original ideas and compositions and browse through additional lessons and tablature online. Download the many backing tracks available and jam along with the Rock House instructors!

Chord Glossary

Here is a collection of new chords for you to learn. Knowing many chords will give you a collection of music building blocks that you can use to learn your favorite songs or write your own masterpiece. Make sure to pick the notes separately first then start strumming away.

C	Cmaj7	C7	C	Csus4
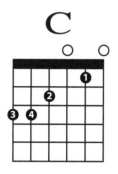	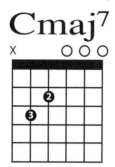	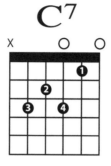	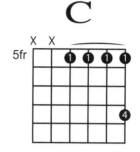	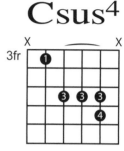

Cmaj7	Cm	Cm7	C7	C9
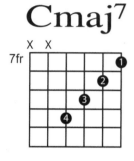	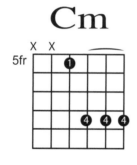	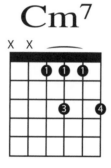	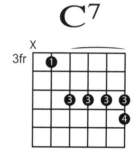	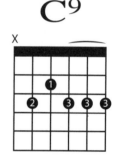

D	Dmaj7	D7	Dsus4	Dmaj7
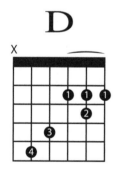	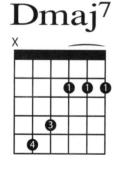	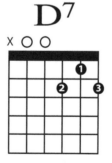	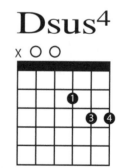	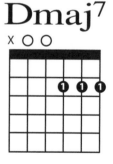

Dm	Dm7	Dm7	D13
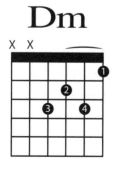	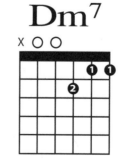	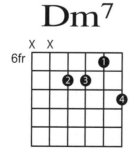	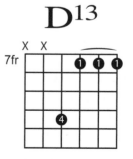

E
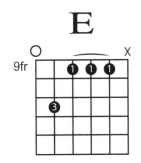

Emaj⁷
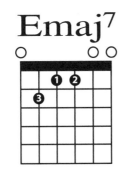

E⁷
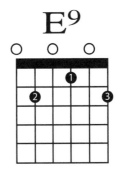

E⁹
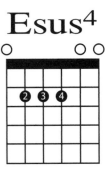

Esus⁴
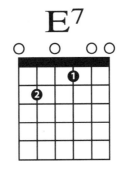

Esus²
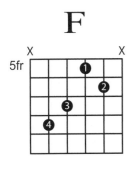

Em⁷
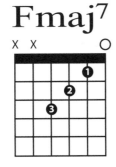

Em⁷
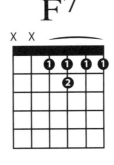

Em⁹
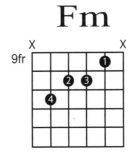

F
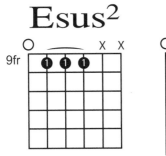

Fmaj⁷
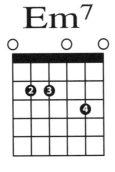

F⁷
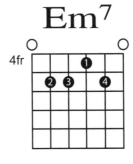

Fm
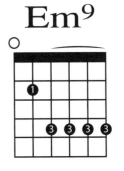

Fm⁷
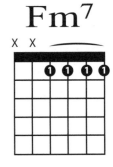

Fm⁷
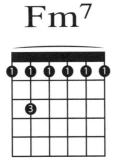

Fsus⁴
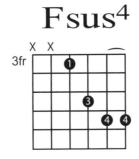

Fm⁶
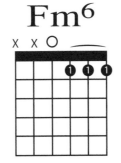

Gmaj⁷

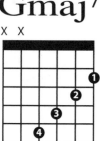

G⁷

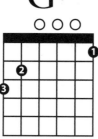

G⁷

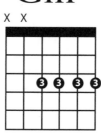

G⁷sus⁴

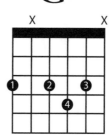

G⁹

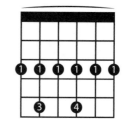

G¹³

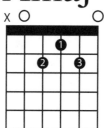

Gm⁷

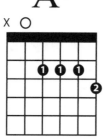

Gm

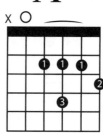

A⁶

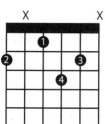

Amaj⁷

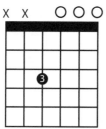

A⁷

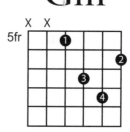

A⁹

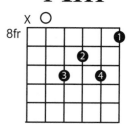

Am

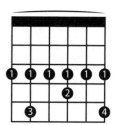

Am⁷

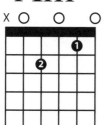

Am⁶

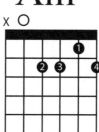

Asus⁴

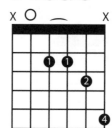

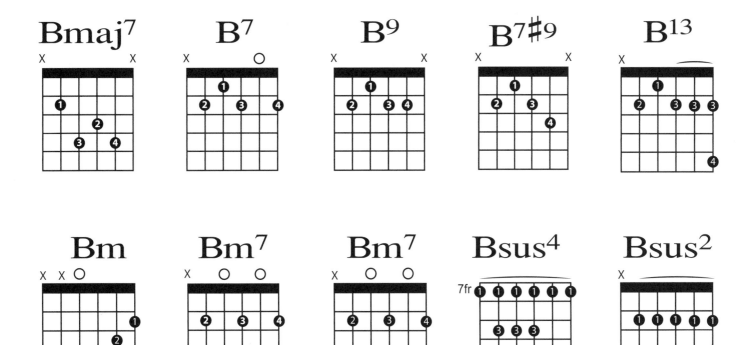

Circle of 4th's and 5th's

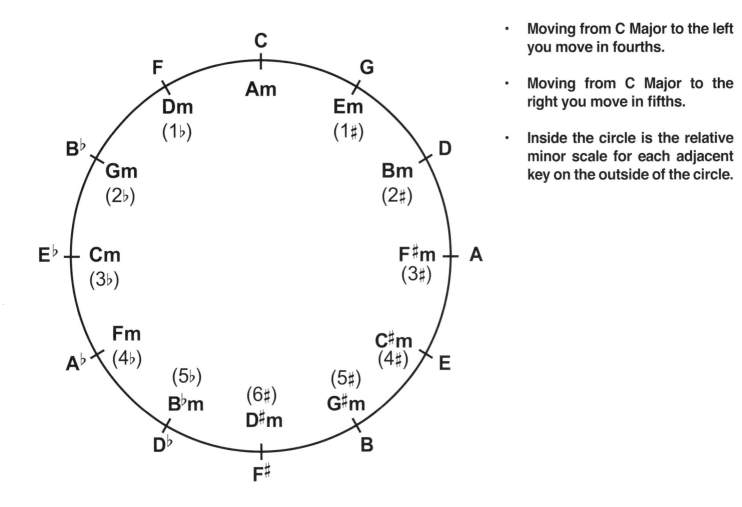

- Moving from C Major to the left you move in fourths.

- Moving from C Major to the right you move in fifths.

- Inside the circle is the relative minor scale for each adjacent key on the outside of the circle.

All Keys Relative Minor

C Major
C D E F G A B C D E F G A
A Minor

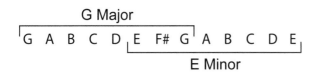

G Major
G A B C D E F# G A B C D E
E Minor

F Major
F G A B♭ C D E F G A B♭ C D
D Minor

D Major
D E F# G A B C# D E F# G A B
B Minor

B♭ Major
B♭ C D E♭ F G A B♭ C D E♭ F G
G Minor

A Major
A B C# D E F# G# A B C# D E F#
F# Minor

E♭ Major
E♭ F G A♭ B♭ C D E♭ F G A♭ B♭ C
C Minor

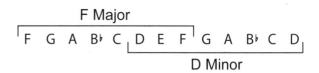

E Major
E F# G# A B C# D# E F# G# A B C#
C# Minor

A♭ Major
A♭ B♭ C D♭ E♭ F G A♭ B♭ C D♭ E♭ F
F Minor

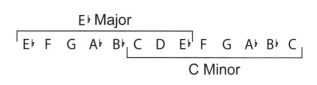

B Major
B C# D# E F# G# A# B C# D# E F# G#
G# Minor

D♭ Major
D♭ E♭ F G♭ A♭ B♭ C D♭ E♭ F G♭ A♭ B♭
B♭ Minor

F# Major
F# G# A# B C# D# E# F# G# A# B C# D#
D# Minor

G♭ Major
G♭ A♭ B♭ C♭ D♭ E♭ F G♭ A♭ B♭ C♭ D♭ E♭
E♭ Minor

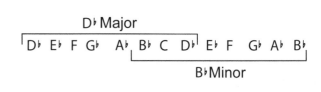

C# Major
C# D# E# F# G# A# B# C# D# E# F# G# A#
A# Minor

C♭ Major
C♭ D♭ E♭ F♭ G♭ A♭ B♭ C♭ D♭ E♭ F♭ G♭ A♭
A♭ Minor

Full Major Scales

A Major

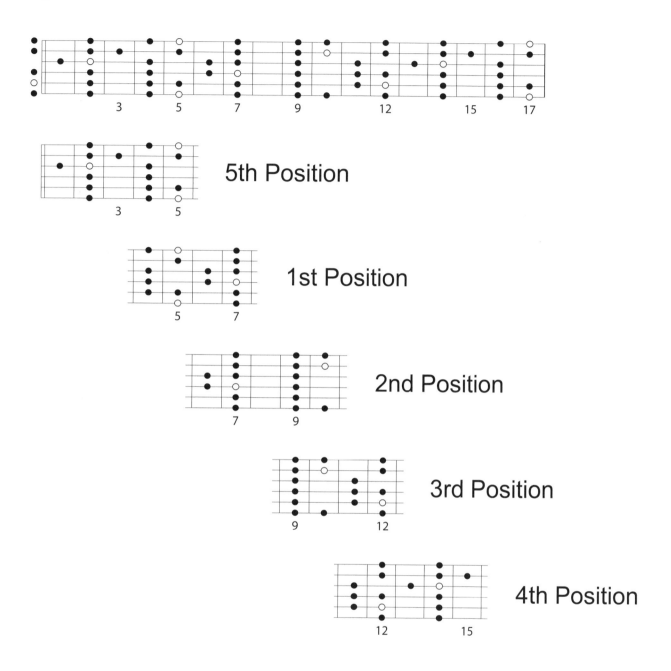

5th Position

1st Position

2nd Position

3rd Position

4th Position

Major Pentatonic Scales

A Major

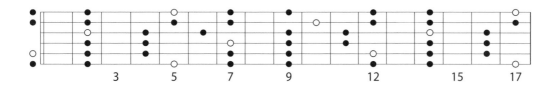

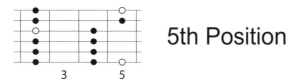

5th Position

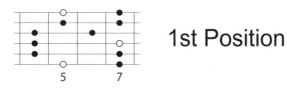

1st Position

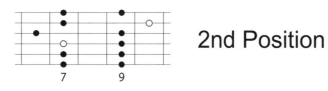

2nd Position

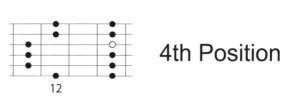

3rd Position

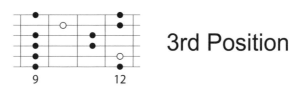

4th Position

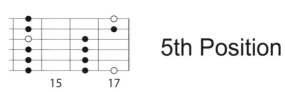

5th Position

Three Note Per String Minor Scales

A Minor

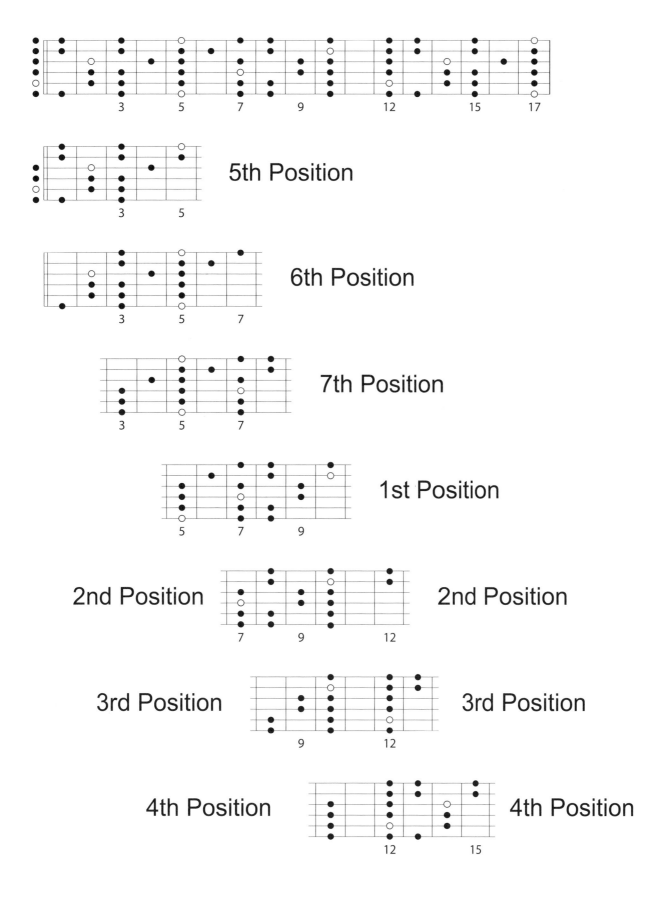

Minor Pentatonic Scales

A Minor

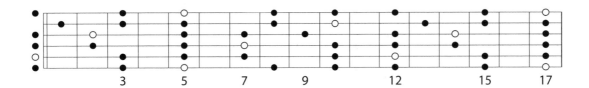

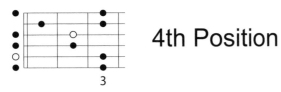

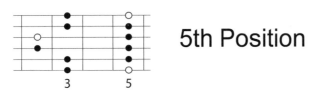

4th Position

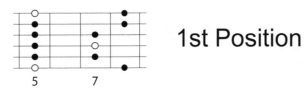

5th Position

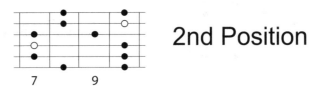

1st Position

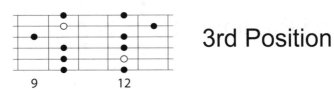

2nd Position

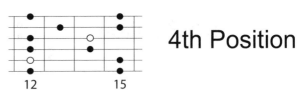

3rd Position

4th Position

JOHNNY BLUES

*Here's the first part of the inspirational piece "Johnny Blues" from my CD, **Drive**. This is a perfect example of how some of the best melodies can be suprisingly easy to play. The audio for this section is available on the included CD. You can also download this track as well as other songs from **Drive** at www.rockhousemethod.com.*

- John McCarthy

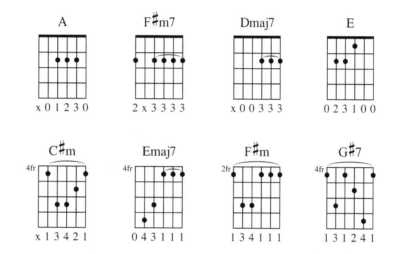

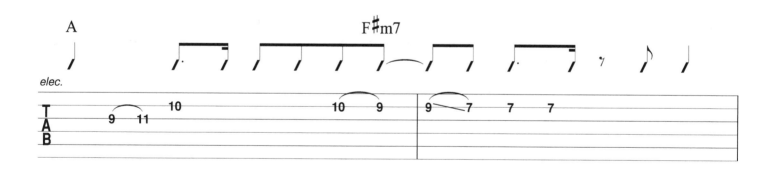

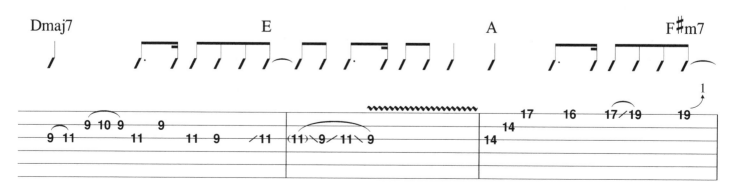

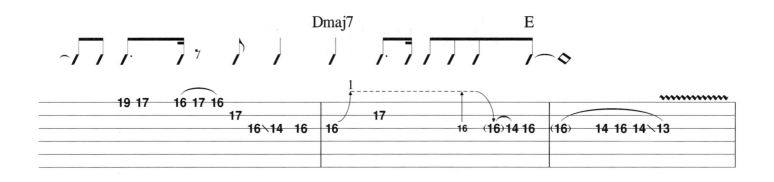

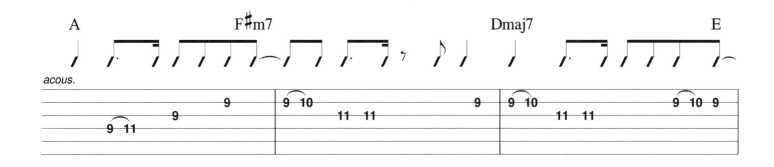

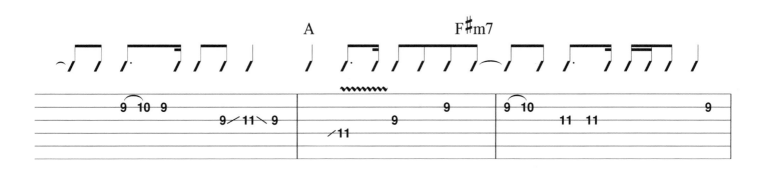

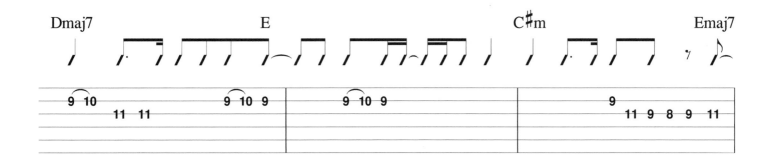

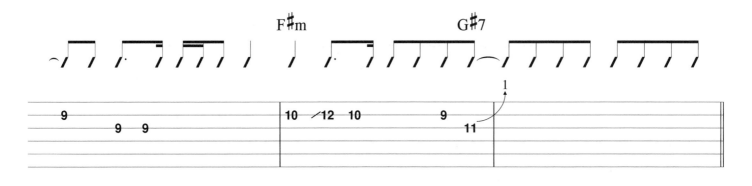

CROSSWORD PUZZLE

Find the famous guitarists that played the songs listed below

Answers on page 79

Across

1. WELCOME TO THE JUNGLE
6. LUCILLE
8. I LOVE ROCK AND ROLL
9. PURPLE HAZE
10. MORE THAN A FEELING
11. IRON MAN
15. ERUPTION
16. KILLING IN THE NAME OF
18. SATISFACTION
19. CAT SCRATCH FEVER
20. REBEL YELL
23. WALK THIS WAY
25. PEACE SELLS
26. FRANKENSTEIN
31. SURRENDER
32. CROSSFIRE
33. MY GENERATION
34. SMOKE ON THE WATER
35. STAIRWAY TO HEAVEN

Down

2. ENTER SANDMAN
3. SURFING WITH THE ALIEN
4. SMELLS LIKE TEEN SPIRIT
5. DETROIT ROCK CITY
7. LIGHT MY FIRE
10. LIVIN' ON A PRAYER
12. MAGIC MAN
13. SUGAR MAGNOLIA
14. TAXMAN
17. PURPLE RAIN
21. BLACK MAGIC WOMAN
22. GO YOUR OWN WAY
24. HIGHWAY TO HELL
27. CRAZY TRAIN
28. TUSH
29. LAYLA
30. KISS ME DEADLY
34. JOHNNY B. GOODE

WORD SEARCH

Find the 14 parts of the acoustic guitar listed in Chapter 1
Answers on page 79

```
X T A E Q Q D P N H J S Q A W K K Y A I
V B V H L Y I I P P T X V F F U F F J V
R R B E C O M C Z O G S W I Z O F J Q E
Y I U A D H O K N S Q N W Z B G T J T Z
Q D D D Y V G G I D B P F S U W S Y N N
N G E S E R O U O T X Z N X T Y W O B V
Z E Q T Z D O A X I H G U V R C G U R V
B P B O T H F R M O M V T S A B B N I F
L I R C G H G D G N A N Z L P F X D D V
L N Q K C N E C K M C Y U K B C Z H G A
K S B K C P G K S A H P N R U S N O E V
W A O O S D N H T R I O D H T W D L V H
J D B F N B C X I K N X M V T O Q E M Q
X D X Y R C K I M E E J S V O Q Z A U W
X L M Z Q E W I T R H C D N N U I U X N
M E K T C M T H N S E J M W O D P C N D
Z Q Q X B X C S T Q A W Q E Z W N O G N
F R E T B O A R D B D U Y M Q F X U G C
T R B A Q R D U M G S R W A S U D Z Q L
R X X S N F Z Y F R J H B A F W P Q U W
```

78

Crossword and Word Search Answer Keys

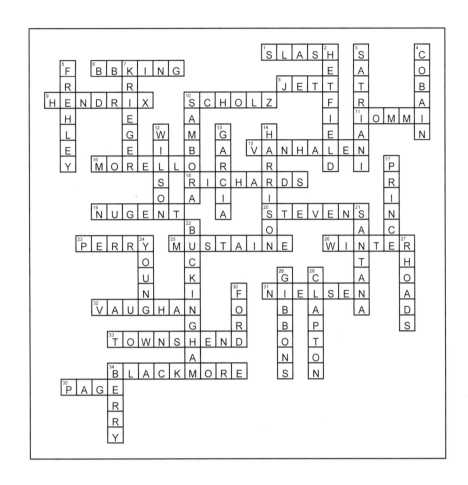

Acoustic Guitar Accessories

Strings & Picks

Strings and picks are both available in different gauges. Heavier gauge strings produce a thicker, fuller sound; lighter gauges are thinner, easier to bend, and great for soloing. There are many different types of picks in different thicknesses. A heavy pick may offer you more control for lead playing, but medium and light picks have a flexibility that's good for rhythm playing. A fingerpick is a type of ring that you wear on your thumb for downpicking, allowing all of your fingers to be available for more complex fingerpicking. When changing your strings, you'll probably want to use a string winder. A string winder is a simple gadget that fits right over the machine heads so that you can quickly wind or unwind a string.

String winder

Music Stands & Metronomes

As soon as you begin your first guitar lesson, you'll notice how important it is to have a music stand. Whenever you try to learn a new song from sheet music, or even go through a lesson in this book, you'll want to have the music right in front of you where it's close and easy to read. Don't try to balance a book on your lap or read it from the floor. If you're practicing scales and exercises or working out a difficult new guitar line, you can use a metronome to set a steady practice tempo and keep yourself in time. There are mechanical or electronic models, or you can download the free one from www.rockhousemethod.com and use your computer to keep time.

Electronic pocket metronome

Capos & Slides

A capo is a moveable clamp that attaches to the neck of the guitar and barres across all six strings. Whichever fret the capo is placed at can then be thought of as the nut; the capo transposes the entire guitar to that position, making it possible to play all of the open chords there. Many acoustic players prefer the full open chord sound and use capos almost exclusively. Capos are popular at the 1st, 2nd, 3rd, 5th and 7th frets, but you can place a capo anywhere at all on the neck. A capo at the 12th fret transposes the guitar one octave higher and gives it a bright, mandolin tone.

A capo is clamped to the neck.

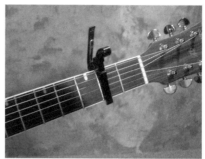

Capo properly placed at the 2nd fret.

An essential element of the blues guitar sound is the slide. A slide is a sleeve (usually glass) that fits over the ring finger of your left hand. With a slide you can slide notes or chords in a steady, smooth motion, making the guitar "talk." Slide guitar is also very popular in many rock styles, and can be heard in songs like "Freebird" and "Bad to the Bone."

A slide can be worn on your ring finger.

Pickups & Effects

If your acoustic guitar is an electric-acoustic, it already has a pickup in it. If not, you can get a separate pickup that attaches to the guitar's sound hole. In basic terms, a pickup is like the guitar's microphone; the vibrations from the strings are magnetically picked up and turned into a signal that you can plug into an amp or PA system. An acoustic guitar doesn't need to be plugged in for you to hear it, but once it is, you can add effects like reverb, chorus, even distortion. With newer USB converters and software, you can also plug your guitar into a computer and play your way through cyberspace. Just connect right to your pc and you can get access to a whole arsenal of software featuring guitar effects, amp sounds, interactive lessons and virtual recording studios.

Tuners

An electronic tuner is a necessity for any gigging guitarist, and tuners have become so common that they're often included in other effects units. Tuners are also sometimes put right into a guitar's electronics. If you don't have a tuner, you can download the free online tuner at our support website.

Straps

Acoustic guitar straps can attach at the body if there's a strap button there. If not, a strap can be tied to the headstock between the nut and the machine heads. Straps come in a variety of materials and styles. When picking out a strap, try to find one that's both comfortable and that looks good with your guitar. Also available are strap locks (locking buttons that will keep the strap secured to the guitar).

Cords

Investing a few dollars more to get a nice, heavy duty guitar cord is worthwhile. The cheaper ones don't last very long, while a professional quality cable can work perfectly for years. Some of the better cords even include a lifetime warranty. Cords also come in a variety of lengths, gauges and colors.

Cases & Stands

The two main types of guitar cases are hardshell cases and softshell cases. Hardshell cases are more expensive and have a sturdy construction designed for maximum protection during travel. A much lighter and smaller alternative to the traditional guitar case is a gig bag: a padded, zippered guitar glove that is carried over the shoulders like a backpack. Guitar stands are usually collapsible and easy to take with you, but you can also use one at home to keep your guitar on display when you're not practicing.

Make Your Own Tool Kit

Put together your own tool kit by keeping all of the important tools and spare parts you need in one place, like a small backpack or a compartment inside your guitar case. You should always have spare strings, a string winder, picks, batteries, and any small screwdrivers or wrenches that fit your guitar. You can purchase a multipurpose tool designed especially for guitarists (sort of like a pocket knife without the knife) that contains a few different types of screwdrivers and an assortment of allen wrenches. Some other good things to keep with you: wire cutters, fuses if your amp uses them, guitar polish and a soft cloth, music paper and pencil, and duct tape. You may also want to keep a small recording device handy to record your own musical ideas and use them to start writing your own songs.

Changing a String

Old guitar strings may break or lose their tone and become harder to keep in tune. You might feel comfortable at first having a teacher or someone at a music store change your strings for you, but eventually you will need to know how to do it yourself. Changing the strings on a guitar is not as difficult as it may seem and the best way to learn how to do this is by practicing. Guitar strings are fairly inexpensive and you may have to go through a few to get it right the first time you try to restring your guitar. How often you change your strings depends entirely on how much you play your guitar, but if the same strings have been on it for months, it's probably time for a new set.

Most strings attach at the headstock in the same way, however electric and acoustic guitars vary in the way in which the string is attached at the bridge. Before removing the old string from the guitar, examine the way it is attached to the guitar and try to duplicate that with the new string. Acoustic guitars often use removeable bridge pins that fasten the end of the string to the guitar by pushing it into the bridge and securing it there.

Follow the series of photos below for a basic description of how to change a string. Before trying it yourself, read through the quick tips for beginners on the following page.

Use a string winder to loosen the string.

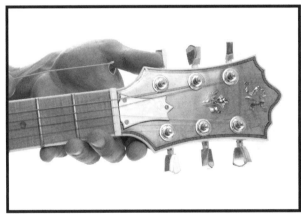

Remove the old string from the tuning post.

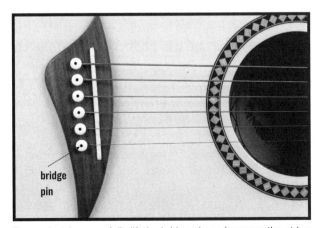

For each string, carefully lift the bridge pin and remove the string from the guitar. Set the pin aside and discard the string.

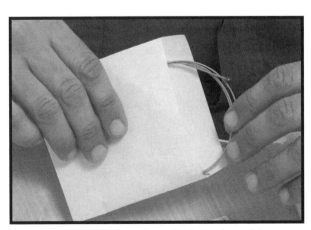

Remove the new string from the packaging and uncoil it.

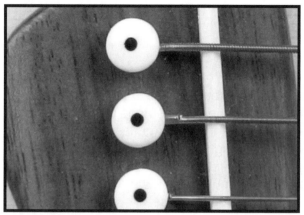

Thread the end of the new string over the nut and place the end of the string in the groove on the bridge pin. Carefully push the pin back into the bridge to lock the string in place.

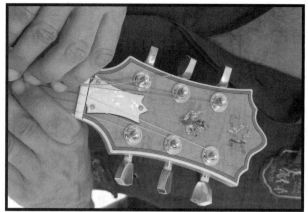

Pull the string along the neck and thread it through the small hole on the tuning post.

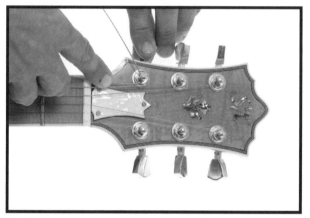

Hold the string in place just after the nut with your finger and tighten up the slack in the string with the machine head.

Carefully tighten the string and tune it to the proper pitch.

You can cut the old string off the guitar but you may want to unwind it instead and save it as a spare in case you break a string later.

Check to make sure you have the correct string in your hand before putting it on the guitar. The strings may be color coded at the end to help you identify them.

Be sure to wind the string around the tuning post in the proper direction (see photos), and leave enough slack to wind the string around the post several times. The string should wind around the post underneath itself to form a nice, neat coil.

Once the extra slack is taken up and the string is taught, tune it very gradually to pitch, being careful not to overtighten and accidentally break the new string.

Once the string is on the guitar and tightened up, you can cut the excess string sticking out from the tuning post with a wire cutter. The sharp tail end that is left can be bent downward with the wire cutter to get it out of the way and avoid cutting or stabbing your finger on it.

Check the ends of the string to make sure it is sitting correctly on the proper saddle and space on the nut.

New strings will go out of tune very quickly until they are broken in. You can gently massage the new string with your thumbs and fingers once it's on the guitar, slightly stretching the string out and helping to break it in. Then retune the string and repeat this process a few times for each string.

our roots

House of Blues is a home for live music and southern-inspired cuisine in an environment celebrating the African American cultural contributions to blues music and folk art. In 1992, our company converted an historical house in Cambridge, Massachusetts into the original House of Blues®. The original House of Blues opened its doors on Thanksgiving Day, 1992 feeding the homeless before opening to the public. Our commitment to serving the community will always be a priority.

We now have the pleasure of bringing live music to 16 major markets in the U. S. and Canada through our 10 club and 19 arena and amphitheatre venues. Come share the House of Blues experience. Get intimate with your favorite band in our Music Hall or enjoy soulful sounds and eats at our popular weekend Gospel Brunch. Savor down home, southern inspired cooking in the restaurant. Be a VIP for an exclusive night out in the membership club Foundation Room. Celebrate an important event in one of our cool private party rooms and take home a special souvenir from our retail store. We look forward to welcoming you to our house!

our mission

To create a profitable, principled global entertainment company.
To celebrate the diversity and brotherhood of world culture.
To promote racial and spiritual harmony through love, peace, truth,
   righteousness and non-violence.

musical diversity

In our Music Halls, you will find almost every music genre imaginable. Rock n' Roll, Punk, Alternative, Heavy Metal, Rap, Country, Hip-Hop, Rhythm and Blues, Rock en Español, Jazz, Zydeco, Folk, Electronica and many other genres grace our stages. We welcome and celebrate music as a form of art and expression.

Music is a celebration. We design and manage venues with the complete experience in mind. *Best Outdoor Venue. Theatre of the Year. Arena/Auditorium of the Year. Best Large Outdoor Concert Venue. Best Live Music Club of the Year. Talent Buyer of the Year.* From large amphitheatres and arenas to small clubs, our venues and staff garner industry accolades year after year. View our upcoming shows, buy tickets and register for presales and special offers at www.hob.com.

The Gorge Amphitheatre is located in George, WA and has been voted Best Outdoor Arena several years running.

the visual blues

The House of Blues' walls feature American folk art affectionately referred to as the visual blues. With over a thousand original pieces of folk art, House of Blues houses one of the largest publicly displayed folk art collections in America. Like music, these pieces represent a form of artistic expression available to everyone.

philanthropy

Throughout our support of the International House of Blues Foundation (IHOBF), over 50,000 students and teachers experience the Blues SchoolHouse program in our music halls annually. This program explores the history, music and cultural impact of the blues and related folk art through live music, narration and a guided tour of our folk art collection. The program highlights African American cultural contributions and emphasizes the importance of personal expression. The IHOBF is dedicated to promoting cultural understanding and creative expression through music and art (www.ihobf.org).